Global
Simulation Models

Global
Simulation Models
A Comparative Study

John Clark and Sam Cole
with
Ray Curnow and Mike Hopkins
Science Policy Research Unit,
University of Sussex

A Wiley–Interscience Publication

JOHN WILEY & SONS
London · New York · Sydney · Toronto

Copyright © 1975, by John Wiley & Sons, Ltd.

All rights reserved.

No part of this book may be reproduced by any means, nor
transmitted, nor translated into a machine language without the written permission of the publisher.

Library of Congress Cataloging in Publication Data:

Clark, John
Global simulation models—a comparative study

A Wiley–Interscience publication.
1. Economic forecasting—Mathematical models.
2. Computer simulation. I. Cole, Sam, joint
author. II. Brighton, Eng. University of Sussex.
Science Policy Research Unit. III. Title.
HB3730.C54   338.5′442   74–32231

ISBN 0 471 15899 2
Photosetting by Thomson Press (India) Limited, New Delhi
and Printed in Great Britain by Pitman Press, Bath, Avon

Preface

Few academic debates in recent years have been as heated as that surrounding the use of computer simulation models for studying the problems and future of mankind. The advocates of such models have, in many cases, proclaimed their emergence as a revolutionary breakthrough in aiding man's efforts to understand the forces that influence physical and social processes; their opponents, often with great ferocity and bitterness, have rejected these models as being at best useless and at worst positively dangerous.

As is frequently the case in situations which become polarized in this way, the issues involved are not simple, or easily separated from one another. Differences of opinion are therefore to be expected and indeed welcomed. It is clear from much that has been written on the subject, however, that missionary zeal and academic jealousy have played their part, and lack of technical knowledge and misunderstandings are frequently in evidence. This book represents an attempt to clarify many of the issues involved in the use of computer models for forecasting.

It is hoped that the book will be of value to two groups of people in particular: first, those currently engaged in computer modelling work who wish to gain a wider view of the potential and limitations of social-system modelling and, secondly, those who have an interest in futures studies and a desire to appreciate the extent to which computer models can be of assistance in understanding and anticipating events and processes that can be of great importance to the future of mankind.

The early part of the book is devoted to a discussion of the background to the recent interest in global forecasting and a description of world computer models, the first of which was constructed by Forrester in 1971. This historical survey includes discussions of the claims made for these models, the major criticisms of them and their impact on Governments and the public.

A thorough evaluation of the role of computer models requires that we consider the extent to which the ends for which they are constructed are worthwhile, and whether there are viable means of achieving these ends. World models are concerned with problems of a global character and a discussion of what constitutes such problems, and how they are connected, follows. Perceived connections between phenomena lead naturally to the concept of a system, which is closely allied to the use of computer models, and we discuss the ways in which such models can be expected to clarify and permit forecasts to be made of system behaviour. Computer models of world problems are, of course, a relatively new phenomenon, representing a departure from the conventional methods of academic study. They depend to a great extent, however, on the methods used and the degree of development of the major discipline areas, a discussion of which helps to put computer models in context.

To obtain a more complete picture of the 'state-of-the-art' of dynamic global modelling, we discuss the range of tools that the world modeller has at his disposal; the success of any modelling enterprise must depend critically on the potential of these tools, which fall naturally into two main classes. First there are those of a technical nature: are currently available modelling methodologies and computers adequate? Secondly there are those of a logistic nature: are the present stores of data and theory on which modellers are required to draw sufficient for their purposes?

What place should the computer have in the formation of policies which affect the lives of ordinary individuals? This inevitably leads to questions of the conflict between a scientist's academic integrity and his rightful participation in political debate. The remainder of the book is primarily concerned with a discussion of the various aspects of this problem. We examine the case for the use of world models, and models of more modest application, as aids to policy making, both in specific terms (by discussing individual cases) and in a more general way. Overall, our hope is that we are providing evidence which will enable individuals to reach their own conclusions on the place of computer simulation models representing important issues in both academic and public domains.

It is appropriate here to give a brief history of the interest and involvement of the Science Policy Research Unit in these matters and of the development of this book. The Unit has, for several years, been concerned with the study of interdisciplinary forecasting and planning at industrial, national and international levels. After the publication of *The Limits to Growth* by Meadows in 1972, it was decided that, in view of the profound impact of this work, a comprehensive review should be undertaken by the Unit; this resulted in the publication of *Thinking About the Future*, which discussed in depth the underlying assumptions and socio-political implications of the Meadows model (Cole and coworkers, 1973). At the beginning of that year, the Unit was awarded a contract by the UK Joint Research Councils to study 'The application of dynamic analysis and forecasting to world problems', the object being to review the current status and potential of computer simulation techniques. This study was carried out by Clark, Cole, Curnow and Hopkins in consultation with Professors Christopher Freeman and Marie Jahoda. During and since the study the authors visited research institutes throughout the world where simulation models of all kinds are being constructed, and attended presentations of the global models described in this book at international meetings; among the more important of these were the presentations of the Mesarovic–Pestel and Bariloche world models at the International Institute for Applied

Systems Analysis in Austria and of the Japanese work at a Club of Rome Symposium in Tokyo. During the summer of 1974, Clark and Cole undertook to rewrite the study in the light of more recent reports and information, using material from the original study. Some of the technical sections and the appendixes were drafted by Curnow and Hopkins who cannot, however, be held responsible for the interpretation of their findings by the authors. Hopkins has now left the Science Policy Research Unit to take up an appointment at the International Labor Organization in Geneva.

ACKNOWLEDGEMENTS

Many individuals have contributed to the ideas contained in this book, both through their readiness to share their thinking and through the provision of research material, often before publication. For this and the hospitality and courtesy shown to us, even when points of view have been quite different, we offer our sincere thanks. That we do not list individuals or organizations is simply because they are too numerous. We would, however, like to pay special tribute to MIT, Bariloche, the Japan Club of Rome, the United Kingdom Department of the Environment, and the Mesarovic–Pestel teams with whom we have had frank and informal discussions on several occasions at Sussex and elsewhere. We would also like to thank our colleagues at the University of Sussex, the United Kingdom Research Councils, the United Kingdom Atomic Energy Authority and Department of Trade and Industry, the Programmes Analysis Unit and the European Commission for funds and support.

Quotations used in this book are reproduced by the permission of: the American Institute of Planners; J. C. K. Ash and W. J. Smyth; Brookings Institution; Anne Chisholm; Council of Europe; Elsevier Scientific Publishing Company; Harper & Row Publishers, Inc.; P. House; Institute of Economic Affairs; IPC Business Press Ltd.; B.O Jansson; Professor Y. Kaya; John Lambert; Suzette McLeod; Professor M. Mesarovic; MIT Press; New Scientist and Jon Tinker; Organisation for Economic Cooperation and Development; Simon Ramo; Professor J. M. Richardson; Sage Publications, Inc.; Scicon Ltd.; Science Journal; Swedish Natural Science Research Council; Time Inc.; Times Newspapers Ltd.; Union of International Associations; University of California Press; Wright Allen Press.

Contents

1

Introduction

CONCERN ABOUT THE FUTURE

Concern with the kind of issues dealt with in global forecasting models is not new. In his essay *A Summary View of the Principle of Population*, published in 1830, the economist Thomas Malthus predicted that economic growth would be restricted by the difficulty of finding sufficient food. Any short-term increase in affluence would, Malthus asserted, bring about an increase in population which would in the long term merely maintain average *per capita* consumption.

Later in the nineteenth century, pessimistic views of the world's social future were reflected in literature, for example in H. G. Well's *The Time Machine*. Early in the twentieth century the publication of Huxley's *Brave New World* and Orwell's *1984* emphasized the trend against the view that technology would lead to an ideal society, which had been prevalent at the time of the Industrial Revolution and had been illustrated much earlier in works such as More's *Utopia*. It had become clear that, contrary to the beliefs of the earlier optimists, there was no reason to believe that technology, although capable of greater things than Malthus thought possible, would always be used for the benefit of mankind.

On the more local level, documented interest in the quality of the immediate environment existed in England as far back as the thirteenth century, when attempts were made to control pollution in London. Several vivid accounts exist of the state of air pollution, particularly in northern English towns, shortly after the Industrial Revolution and it is reasonable to assume from these that the condition of the atmosphere over towns has been far better in recent years. It seems, however, that preventive measures were only considered justifiable if the pollution was such as to cause death or the spread of epidemic diseases. More recently, rather less severe criteria have been used to justify the introduction of legislation, for example the Clean Air Acts of the UK in 1956.

It is pertinent to ask why, in view of the above, such issues have captured the public imagination again in the last few years and, particularly, to enquire into the reasons for the recent rise of 'environmentalist' movements which have been important influences on the authors of the models described in this book. The development of atomic and nuclear weapons effectively destroyed the notion that science and technology were benign fairy-godmothers capable only of ameliorating problems. Further, the existence of the Bomb, a sword of Damocles apparently capable of extinguishing the human race, gave rise to understandable feelings of fatalism and insecurity and to concern for the future of the planet as a whole. Improvements in communications have ensured that examples of the pernicious effects of technology, such as the toxic effects of DDT and heavy metals, have become widely known, especially as such subjects are favourites with the media. Further, now that the majority of people in the developed countries are no longer concerned solely with their personal day-to-day existence, they have time to reflect on longer-term issues, particularly the cost of their affluence, in terms of pollution and depletion of natural resources, and the increase in population.

The modern environmentalist movement is certainly of longer standing and has pursued its ends with greater fervour in the USA than elsewhere in the developed world, possibly because of the relative failure of the United States social system to establish planning controls and social services of the type long familiar to Europeans (Sinclair, 1973). The movement can perhaps be dated from the publication of Rachel Carson's *Silent Spring* in 1962, which was the first popular account of the dangerous effects of pesticides on wild life. The book had a mixed reception, being attacked particularly by the chemical companies, but did give rise to high-level discussions on pesticides policy (Graham, 1970). As the environmentalist cause gained momentum, the status of ecologists rose in public esteem. Although the word 'ecology' has existed for almost a century, ecologists were previously regarded as harmless, rather eccentric nature-lovers; almost overnight they became sages on whose wisdom the salvation of the human race depended. Many ecologists resented this sudden popularization of their science, but it is true to say that others welcomed it and added fuel to the movement. Kenneth Mellanby has said, 'The trouble is that some ecologists, and some of the people who like to be called ecologists, but who are really publicists without any particular knowledge of the subject, feel they can get a better hearing by saying everything is getting worse all the time' (Chisholm, 1972). In any case, the pessimistic literature proliferated, Ehrlich's *The Population Bomb* and Commoner's *The Closing Circle* being outstanding bestsellers.

Despite the fact that the word was in use in the 1870s, ecology first became widely discussed in the UK largely as a result of the Reith Lectures delivered in the Autumn of 1969 by Sir Frank Fraser Darling. During these lectures Mr Reginald Maudling, a Shadow Minister, asked if someone could tell him: what *was* ecology? If the word was not in general use at that time, it quickly became familiar and the Government established a Royal Commission on Environmental Pollution and an Environment Ministry (Chisholm, 1972).

In the last few years, the connection between environmental issues and many problems of great importance to the future of mankind, such as population increase, urbanization, malnourishment, natural resource depletion and international conflict have become more apparent. There is growing concern in all developed countries where the goal of unbridled economic growth is less widely accepted as being realistic or desirable. With this interest among officials, academics and laymen, it is not surprising that an increasing volume of work has begun in an attempt to remove some of the uncertainty regarding the future and the impact that man can have in shaping it.

As the world becomes 'smaller', the actions of one government are, through expanding world trade and international communications, becoming increasingly likely to affect other nations, and there is a growing realization that much more attention should be paid to understanding the repercussions of manoeuvres which attempt to ameliorate specific problems. Because it is widely felt that the problems are so complex and strongly interrelated and cannot realistically be studied in isolation, the 'systems approach' has been widely advocated and we now move on to consider its rise in popularity.

THE SYSTEMS VIEWPOINT

The 'systems approach' to the study of a problem or situation involves the consideration of the many interrelated features of the problem simultaneously, rather than the study of each facet in isolation. The belief that it is useful rests on the obvious importance of interactions between component parts of many real-world issues (Jenkins, 1969).

Like environmentalism, the systems approach to problem solving has a long history but has recently been the subject of a great upsurge of interest. Its roots can be found in the writings of ancient philosophers, who considered the question of 'holism', a concept which arises from the observation that 'the whole is greater than the sum of the parts'. A rather trivial example of this is that the motion of two neighbouring heavenly bodies cannot be explained by studying each in isolation, but only by considering both simultaneously and including their mutual interaction (and possibly those of other bodies also). In general, the concept implies that interactions are strong between the components of the entity being studied and that useful results can only be achieved using an 'overall' rather than a 'piecemeal' approach, despite the greater complexity of the former.

The use of the term 'systems engineering' by many authors (e.g. Jenkins (1969), Checkland (1971)) implies that the subject generally has a scientific connotation. People who have attempted to analyse human situations from a systems point of view, using rational methods, have frequently been labelled as 'technocrats'. An early proponent of the 'technocratic' outlook was Thorstein Veblen, who, early in this century, contrasted the businessman, whose actions were dictated by financial motives and were contrary to the interests of society, with the engineer, whose only concern was to ensure the smooth running of the economic machine. Understandably, Veblen's ideas received a good deal of support during the Great Depression of the 1930s, in particular in the form of a group formed under Howard T. Scott. Scott's group, however, was not a success and was quickly disbanded (Simmons, 1973).

The modern systems approach is a direct descendant of operations research, which emerged in its present form during the Second World War. Previous military experience was of no relevance to many new weapons and weapon systems. Physicists, biologists, mathematicians and other specialists were brought in by the British Government to help devise strategy for incorporating new equipment into the air defence system. Subsequently, similar methods were used in the US space programme and operations research was employed to a very great extent to assist company managers.

In 1954, four well known scientists, Bertalanffy, Boulding, Gerard and Rapoport, founded the Society for General Systems Research in the USA. The society, which is primarily composed of academics, still flourishes. Its aims are to promote systems thinking by developing methodologies for the analysis and design of large man-made systems, with a view to gaining insights into the structure and functioning of the whole range of system types. Particular emphasis is laid on the need to develop general theories and concepts which, it is hoped, will serve to unify the present fragmented aspect of the various sciences. The value of 'interdisciplinary' research is stressed and the Society provides a means for 'systems thinkers' working in particular academic disciplines to exchange ideas and work towards a general systems science. A UK branch of the Society was set up in 1969 and there are a number of affiliated societies on the continent of Europe.

Perhaps the biggest impetus to the rise of the modern 'systems movement' was provided by the rapid development of the electronic computer since the Second World War. This development meant that, for the first time, it was feasible to study the dynamic behaviour of complex interacting systems, provided that appropriate parameters could be identified, quantified and related to one another. Its use is illustrated by the 'system dynamics' approach developed in the USA. One of the first applications of system dynamics was to a description of the functioning of industrial concerns by the Sloan School of Management at MIT, under the direction of Jay W. Forrester. Forrester's book *Industrial Dynamics* was published in 1962. Despite criticisms, many people were attracted to the idea of system dynamics, which appeared to offer a simple method of representing a wide variety of systems in quantitative form. It began to be used widely in industrial and other fields. Forrester himself widened his area of application to urban studies (*Urban Dynamics*, 1969) and the entire world, *World Dynamics* (Forrester, 1971a). There are now few subjects which have not been explored to some extent with the aid of the computer.

The far-reaching and interwoven nature of policy issues has led to the belief that the systems approach might be of benefit in the field of Government planning. There is a good deal of heated controversy as to what extent this is likely to be true. The value of its present use in the military field is emphasized by Ways (1962):

The kind of defense planning now being done requires much sharper definition of war aims than has characterised American policy-making in past conflicts. Just as 'drop-in-the-bucket' comments make for sloppy thinking in domestic policy, so absolutist concepts of 'total victory' and 'unconditional surrender' and 'all-out effort' and 'peace at any price' induce a kind of foreign policy thinking that can alternate disastrously between the poles of apathetic inaction and apocalyptic commitment. McNamara, his systems analysts, and their computers are not only contributing to the practical effectiveness of US actions, but raising the moral level of policy by a more conscious and selective attention to the definition of its aims.*

Effective selling of such ideas by analysts, and possibly desperation by politicians, led to the creation of the 'moon-ghetto' metaphor stated by Vice-President Hubert H. Humphrey in a speech at the Smithsonian Institution and quoted in *Aerospace Technology*, vol. 21, May 20 1968:

The techniques that are going to put a man on the Moon are going to be exactly the techniques that we are going to need to clean up our cities; the management techniques that are involved, the coordination of government and business, of scientist and engineer. We're not going to make these cities over just by a speech. And we're not going to do it either just because we have a hundred billion dollars that somebody wants to put into it. I get on my favorite topic: It takes more than just money to do anything. It requires knowledge, planning; it requires the technology, the ability to get things done. There is no checkbook answer to the problems of America. There are some human answers and the *systems analysis approach* that we have used in our Defense department; ... that is the approach that the modern city of America is going to need if it's going to become a livable social institution. So maybe we're pioneering in space only to save ourselves on Earth. As a matter of fact, maybe the nation that puts a man on the Moon is a nation that will put Man on his feet right here on Earth. I think so.

Although there has been a 'backlash' against the rise of systems methods, the systems movement shows no signs of abating. New departments and institutions are being formed, one of the most recent being the International Institute of Applied Systems Analysis in Vienna.

With environmentalism and the wide application of systems analysis both receiving considerable attention, it is not surprising that news of their marriage in the form of the MIT world models was greeted with enormous interest. We now move on to consider these models in some detail.

THE FIRST GENERATION OF WORLD MODELS

The 'first generation' of world models, comprising Forrester's 'World 2' (described in *World Dynamics* (Forrester, 1971a)) and Meadows's 'World 3' (described in *The Limits to Growth* (Meadows and coworkers, 1972)) were both initiated by the Club of Rome, founded in 1968 by an Italian businessman, Aurelio Peccei. Peccei had previously become concerned about the world's major problems, some of which he described in a book entitled *The Chasm Ahead*, which was published in 1969. Peccei assembled an international group of businessmen, academics and industrialists who were interested in taking a global perspective on the problems facing mankind. These people became the founders of the Club of Rome and, after a series of meetings, decided to initiate the so-called 'Project on the predicament of mankind', to examine the issues

*Reproduced by permission of Fortune Magazine; ©1966, Time Inc.

comprising the 'world problematique'; these included such problems as poverty in the midst of plenty, degradation of the environment, loss of faith in institutions, uncontrolled urban spread, insecurity of employment, alienation of youth, rejection of traditional values, and inflation and other monetary and economic disruptions. The proclaimed objectives of the Club of Rome are to stimulate research into the nature and possible resolution of world problems, and to improve communication between administrators and others so that awareness of the situation is enhanced (Peccei, 1973a).

In 1970, Carroll Wilson, a member of the Club, suggested that Jay Forrester, a colleague of his at MIT, be invited to give a presentation of his system dynamics approach to the Club at the Battelle Memorial Institute in Geneva. The idea of using this methodology was favourably received and, immediately after making his presentation, Forrester began work on a world dynamics model. The first version of his model (World 1) evolved on the flight back across the Atlantic. World 2 was completed some three weeks later and, at a meeting at MIT, the Club agreed to try to obtain funds for a more ambitious model, to be regarded as Phase One of the Project on the Predicament of Mankind, to be constructed by a team headed by an associate of Forrester's, Dennis Meadows. $250,000 was obtained from the Volkswagen foundation and *The Limits to Growth* was published a year later.

Gillette (1972) reports that at the Smithsonian première in March, 1972, of *The Limits to Growth*, Peccei explained the appeal of the computer-based project. Says Gillette: 'For two years Club members had plodded quietly from Moscow to Rio, from Stockholm to Washington, seeking out political leaders, appraising them of the dangers ahead'. At the meeting, Peccei stated: 'Our message was received with sympathy and understanding but no action followed. What we needed was a stronger tool of communication to move men on the planet out of their ingrained habits. This is the reason for the MIT study and the book'.*

Although computerized world models do have attraction as a means of propaganda for a point of view, they can be defended as worthwhile pieces of research. The characteristic which distinguishes world models from others is their scope: they purport to represent all the socio-technical systems of the world in sufficient detail for the discussion of long-term global futures. Such models can be regarded as attempting to combine economic, demographic and ecological factors. Researchers building these models argue that by taking into account 'all' relevant issues and all world regions, thus eliminating the need to account for externalities, interactions can be represented and many repercussive (and possibly unexpected) effects are brought to our attention. Although Forrester's model World 2 was an embryonic form of the Meadows model World 3, the two are normally associated together since they consider the same social–technical–natural systems and produce similar results. They differ

---

*From *Science*, vol.175, pp. 1088–1092, 10th March 1972. Reproduced by permission of *Science*, ©1972 by the American Association for the Advancement of Science.

only in minor assumptions and the level of detail; World 3 is some 2 to 3 times larger than World 2, and much more effort has been made to calibrate the former on the basis of existing data. The basic assumptions, the methodology used and the results from the models have been discussed at length elsewhere, for example in *World Dynamics*, *The Limits to Growth* and the SPRU critique *Thinking About the Future* (Cole and coworkers, 1973). It therefore does not seem necessary to go beyond a brief description here.

Both World 2 and World 3 are designed to project, up to the end of the next century, average worldwide values for population, available resources, pollution and agricultural and industrial output, on the basis of current trends. 'Feedback' mechanisms are employed so that a change in one parameter affects others which may, in turn, cause further change in the first. Perhaps the most important assumption is that, since the world is finite, a stock of natural resources remains which, according to World 3, will be expended in 250 years at current usage rates.

Figure 1 (Cole and coworkers, 1973) shows a 'standard run' of World 3, i.e. the projected future assuming no change in the physical or socio-economic relationships that govern the world system at present. As can be seen, a crisis is indicated some time in the next century (Meadows stresses that exact dates cannot be given), with rapid declines in food *per capita* and population. Crises

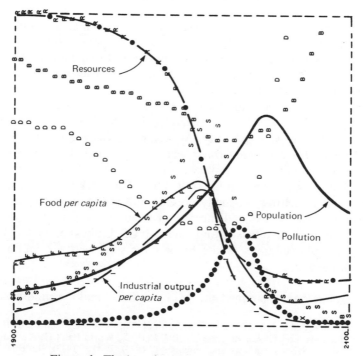

Figure 1. The 'standard run' of the World 3 model

also occur if more optimistic initial values are given to certain parameters; for example, a doubling of assumed resource reserves leads to a very high rise in pollution levels, resulting in a steep decline in population. Even the implementation of policies such as pollution control and birth control do not significantly improve the situation. All these runs show a similar type of behaviour: an exponential growth of population and industrial capital, followed by collapse. Because of delays incorporated in the model, for example between the release of a pollutant and its influence on human health, the 'natural limits' to the earth's carrying capacity can temporarily be exceeded, with disastrous results following. The model indicates a stable future only if very draconian measures, the most important of which are zero increases in population and capital growth, are taken in the very near future.

Publication of the Forrester and the Meadows work stimulated a wide-ranging discussion. The impact of these models may be attributed to a number of reasons:

(1) As we have noted, they came at a time of increasing concern with issues of pollution, famine, overpopulation and, to a lesser extent, resource shortages on a local and global scale.

(2) The use of a 'computer' and computerized output added to the appearance of academic respectability and contributed to an air of objectivity. As indicated earlier, 'technocratic' approaches are particularly acceptable in times of perceived crisis.

(3) The models were constructed at MIT, a very prestigious institution.

(4) The Club of Rome, as an influential and active organization, was an important factor in the initial acceptance of the models (although it must be said that views among the Club's members concerning the issues considered even at that time covered a broad spectrum).

(5) Perhaps the most significant factor, apart from timeliness, was the 'marketing' of *The Limits to Growth* by Potomac Associates who, recognizing a commercial product, gave it wide publicity. According to *Science* (March 10, 1972), 12,000 copies of *The Limits to Growth* were sent to influential government and political leaders, and personal visits were made to them by the Club of Rome members and by Meadows and his colleagues. The work received wide media attention. The model was originally presented at the Smithsonian Institution, to a distinguished invited audience of academics, ambassadors and other high-level government officials, and later at US Embassies in the UK and elsewhere. Popular editions of the book have sold nearly 2 million copies throughout the world.

Many groups have examined the MIT models,* making modifications to

---

*See, for example, that technical discussion in: Dator (1972), Van der Grinten and de Jong (1971), Oerlemans and coworkers (1972), Bray (1972), Boyd (1972), World Bank (1973), Cole and coworkers (1973) and reply (Meadows and coworkers, 1973), Burke (1973), Rademaker (1974), Beckerman (1972), Nordhaus (1973) and reply (Forrester and coworkers, 1974).

illustrate major criticisms. For example, the Sussex group (Cole and coworkers, 1973) developed the Forrester model into a two-region model representing the rich and the poor regions of the world, to demonstrate the weakness of considering merely global averages. The more general technical criticisms of the MIT projects concern:

(1) The assumptions concerning the physical and ecological factors. For example, it is considered that the estimated levels of available non-renewable resources are pessimistic and that insufficient account is taken of probable technological improvements.

(2) The data bases employed. These are thought to be inadequate for the scope of the nominally quantitative model. Many relationships are merely implied from supportive data.

(3) The overemphasis of the physical aspects of world problems without consideration of the technological, sociological, political and psychological changes during the long time-span considered by the projects.

(4) The high degree of aggregation. The world is treated as a whole rather than a system of quite different but interacting political and economic regions.

(5) The mechanistic character of computer models in which all structural relationships are fixed. The results of the computer runs are determined fata·listically only by the choice of the initial or intermediate conditions.

Meadows himself does not deny that many of the points listed above are valid for his model. He has said, for example, that only 0.1% of the data required for a fully satisfactory world model are available. He also stresses that none of his computer runs is a prediction, but rather an indication of the likelihood of 'overshoot and collapse'. Nevertheless, there is, in his statements, a strong implication that the model is sufficiently valid to be of value for policy making.

It is certainly true that the interest shown by academics and the public has been shared by policy makers. Specific policy changes resulting from the models cannot be identified but, in view of widespread attention at government level, some changes in policy perspective have almost certainly occurred. The models and their conclusions have had governmental supporters, if not advocates, in the UK, Europe and the United States. In the UK, the degree of official interest has been sufficient to stimulate the setting up of a government research team charged with the examination of long-term global issues. So it must be said that, as experimental models, they have had exceptional influence.

Tinker (1972) describes UK Government reaction:

A week before the UN Conference on the Human Environment opened in Stockholm, the British Cabinet took a decision which is likely to exert a profound effect on UK domestic and foreign policy. Jay Forrester's report, *World Dynamics*, in late 1971 had a powerful effect in a few areas of Whitehall and Westminster, and the Meadows/MIT study, *Limits to Growth*, has caused a more widespread sense of unease. Even after a series of meetings in which Sir Alan Cottrell, Chief Scientific Adviser to the Cabinet, flew over to Cambridge, Massachusetts, and Meadows came to London to discuss his work with a committee under Cottrell's chairmanship, no clear consensus had appeared in Whitehall. Some of the government's scientific staff—including Cottrell himself and the Department of the Environment's research director, Joe Lyons—were persuaded that the main lines of his conclusions were valid. Others, and these remain in the majority, consider the data and assumptions on which the MIT world model are based to be so inaccurate projections into the future that they cannot be given much credence.

Within the EEC, too, publication of *The Limits to Growth* stimulated a debate sparked off by Mansholt's 'open letter' to the then president of the Community. He takes the study as a starting point for a discussion of future development for the EEC:

Although it is not yet known how exact the calculations are, its general line is already so clear that it can be used as a basis for our discussions and our studies . . .
 Our duty is to point to economic action which can help in limiting births . . . Supposing stable world population, it would seem possible, at least in theory, to bring about a certain equilibrium in the growth of various factors; this is necessary if mankind is to survive (Run V of the MIT Report). (Quoted by Lambert (1972)).*

A further important unofficial citation of *World Dynamics* was in the *Blueprint for Survival*, a document prepared by a large number of influential UK academics calling for an end to economic growth and a long-term reduction in the UK population. The point about this document and Mansholt's letter is certainly not that they are necessarily mistaken in what they are calling for (indeed this is a matter for extended debate), but that they were using the still questionable results of the MIT models as justification or even 'proof' of their position.

Indeed, it is fair to say that, to a considerable extent, reactions to the models depended on preconceived opinions and that they have served to heighten rather than resolve the 'growth–no growth' controversy. Economists in particular have been critical of the models. The bitterness of much of the criticism seems to stem from the perhaps understandable resentment that work of such ambitious scope, attempted on such a flimsy data base, could have such an impact, while economists themselves have spent many years developing techniques and accumulating data for much more limited objectives. In short, they feel that the models are not, and could not be, sound pieces of research. Some, however, feel that economists themselves are to blame for this situation, on the grounds that they have, because of the analytical difficulties involved, chosen to neglect what many people feel to be the most urgent and critical problems.

Today, it is generally agreed that the technical content of the models and their underlying assumptions are weak and that, from this point of view, they were oversold. At the outset, the use of a computer was recognized by the Club of Rome to be a necessary 'vehicle for communication'. Many critics

---

*The Science Policy Research Unit was invited by the European Commission to carry out a feasibility study for a socio-economic model of Europe (Clark and coworkers, 1973 and 1974).

have pointed out that the conclusions of the models are self-evident, given the assumptions, and that the complexity of the models served only to mask this. Yet, many people, including some critics, are of the opinion that the models served a good purpose in stimulating public and academic discussion about important issues. Although not denying the importance of these issues, others would argue that their seriousness was overemphasized and distorted, possibly serving only to cloud more urgent social issues.

THE SCOPE OF THE BOOK

The models we have discussed so far are, at the time of writing (spring 1975), the only world models to have been completed and fully published; but several others are in the course of construction and preliminary reports are available. Although it is impossible to give a complete assessment of these at the present time, it is certainly worthwhile to compare the approaches used with that of the MIT models, as far as is possible on the basis of this information. We will explore the attempts made in these models to overcome some of the criticisms made of the MIT models and then consider the range of techniques open to world modellers.

'Forecasting' is an activity undertaken for many different reasons and the extent to which dynamic modelling, and the world models in particular, can be of value for these purposes will be discussed. We have seen how the MIT models focused attention on those issues which concern the current environmental movements, but will also consider other 'world problems' and assess the contribution that dynamic modelling can make to them.

Many models have been constructed to represent particular issues, and are therefore more restricted in scope than the world models. But even these often deal with matters which cross conventional academic boundaries, which gives rise to a number of problems. An attempt will be made to trace the characteristics of the evolution of knowledge, to describe the basic differences between the academic disciplines and to assess the requirements for satisfactory interdisciplinary research. Some regard the formation of interdisciplinary teams as essential if many outstanding problems are to be studied realistically, while others consider that useful research can only be done by individuals basing their work on techniques developed over many years within a single discipline. The ideal is perhaps a unification of disciplines along the lines of a 'general systems theory' already referred to, but such a theory is currently at a very primitive stage.

Much of the controversy regarding world models is based on a misunderstanding of the potential and limitations of the technical factors. Discussion of them should help to resolve the question whether world models are feasible propositions at the present time and whether the systems approach, with the aid of a computer, really does allow one usefully to 'model anything' or is merely worthless pseudo-science.

In the field of public policy, it is claimed by many of their opponents that computer modellers can do great harm. Models are, it is claimed, crude devices of propaganda masquerading as esoteric pieces of objective scientific research. In a field where values and aspirations play a decisive part, but where the intricacies of computer models are understood by very few, it is suggested by the 'anti-technocrats' that models are a threat to democracy. Sometimes, however, as we have seen in relation to the MIT models, it is acknowledged that models are constructed for the purpose of advocating a particular point of view. The value of this application is discussed and conclusions are reached regarding the value of models in the various roles they can play in the formation of policy.

An attempt to assess the future *of* world models is perhaps as hazardous as attempting to predict the future *with* them. We do have some evidence, however, of their value compared with other forecasting techniques and we have reached some conclusions on their likely future usefulness. We hope that this book will help the reader to do the same.

2

An Overview of New World Modelling Efforts

INTRODUCTION

The 'second generation' of world models were all initiated at more or less the same time and as a reaction to *The Limits to Growth* study. The idea of constructing a 'world model' was quickly taken up by a number of groups; two of the projects described in this chapter, the Mesarovic–Pestel model and the Bariloche Latin American model, were begun as a result of preliminary presentations of World 3 to the Club of Rome, even before *The Limits to Growth* was published.

The new projects often originated as attempts to modify the MIT models so as to take account of their generally recognized defects. In the main, these efforts were soon abandoned since it seemed to be more straightforward to construct entirely new models. The early attempts did serve, however, to illustrate the importance of structural changes in the MIT models, such as dividing them into rich and poor world regions or including technological development functions more responsive to socio-economic determinants. The new models therefore are almost without exception 'disaggregated' into world regions.

Although the models are still designed to relate economic, demographic and ecological factors together in an integrated package, the composition and relationships are, in general, rather more familiar to traditional researchers in these fields than were those of the MIT models. In addition, the models are concerned with somewhat shorter time horizons. The relationship to policy makers and well known ideologies is far more clearly defined, although rather different intentions for their application are presented for the various models. None of the models stress *global physical* limits to growth to the same degree as the MIT group. The questions to be asked of the models relate to the situations of particular blocs of nations, but still in the context of a global framework. Besides changes in the structural and parametric assumptions of the models, in accordance with the underlying motivations of the researchers, the newer models often employ more sophisticated techniques. The MIT models were criticized by systems analysts and modellers for their relative lack of technical sophistication, as well as for their political and theoretical naivety. Many different queries about methodology were raised: the suitability of System Dynamics as a methodology, the apparent need for such big computers, the lack of satisfactory calibration or testing of the model and many others.

It would require several volumes if we were to set out to describe in full detail all features of all models currently under construction. For this detail readers will be referred to appropriate original sources. In any case, most of the models are still evolving and modifications are likely to be made. What we shall provide in this chapter is a description of the main lines of attack which modellers have adopted, the kinds of problems they face and indications of other research which may be pertinent to future efforts. We concentrate the discussion on what we consider to be the most important modelling programs (several of which are associated with the Club of Rome's 'Project on the predicament of mankind'). These illustrate a wide range of the total spectrum of modelling techniques available. Many of the issues raised will then be discussed in more detail in the remainder of the book, other models of interest being referred to where appropriate.

THE CLUB OF ROME/MESAROVIC–PESTEL
STRATEGY FOR SURVIVAL MODEL

The largest second generation model to be developed so far (some 200 times bigger than the MIT models) and the first to be presented to an audience outside the Club of Rome is the model of Mesarovic and Pestel. This study is the major new modelling project of the Club and was initiated after it became obvious that the MIT World 3 model would be deficient in at least three respects (high aggregation, mechanistic approach and limitation to physical aspects). The project is intended to offer an alternative approach to that of MIT, with the object of developing a computer-based planning and decision tool which can be used to analyse world problems and to assess alternative policies and strategies for implementation. The model is an attempt to include both a representation of causal mechanisms operating in the world, and a device for permitting alternative global objectives to be inserted. In the model, the world system is represented in terms of interacting regions with provisions made to investigate any individual country or subregion in the context of regional and global development. The world system is represented by ten regions: North America, Latin America, Western Europe, Eastern Europe, Japan, Australia and South Africa, Middle East and North Africa, Rest of Africa, South and South East Asia, and China (Mesarovic, 1973b). This representation is flexible; extension to a country level of description has been contemplated, although for some purposes fewer than ten regions are used.

The model has two 'levels'. On the macro level, the model of each region includes the gross regional product, total imports and exports, capital and labour productivity and various components of final demand such as public consumption, government expenditure, and total investment. On the micro level, eight production sectors are recognized: agriculture, manufacturing, food processing, energy, mining, services, banking and trade, and residential construction. An input–output framework is used to handle the intermediate demands and a full-scale micro trade matrix will eventually be developed. So far the underlying structure of this economic trade and development model has been developed, but is in a schematic form represented by a one sector economy only for each world region (Blankenship and coworkers, 1974). The structural assumptions used in representing each region vary; for example, total exports of the developed market economies are demand-determined by the import functions of other economies, whereas exports of centrally planned and developing country economies are supply-determined within their own economies. Thus to extrapolate projections of the model in order to examine a transition phase in world development would require certain changes in its structural relationships. Complementary to this single-sector trade model is an attempt to calibrate a production function for each total economy.

The economic model forms the core of the total world model and is intended to provide input to a series of subsystem models including demographic, material and agricultural factors. For example, an energy model will estimate, for each region, the consumption and production of energy, and interregional exchange of energy resources, as a function of economic factors. Energy is treated in both aggregate terms and in reference to individual energy sources, namely solid fuel, liquid fuel, nuclear, gas and hydroelectricity.

Similarly, a world population model has been constructed using the same regions as the economic model. According to early reports, it was intended that, in each region, the population structure would be represented by four age groups with appropriate delays to make possible both an assessment of population 'momentum' and the likely effectiveness of implementation of various population control measures. It was found, however, that the results were only stable if the populations were divided into one year cohorts and it appears that this is the current level of disaggregation.

A food production and arable land use model has been constructed, which allows the assessment of a number of food related issues, including, for example, the need and availability of phosphorus required for intensive agriculture and the consequences of timing and magnitudes of natural disasters such as drought or crop failure due to disease. Once again, a high level of division has been selected: 23 foodstuffs (including honey) are distinguished, although to make this level of division sensible will clearly ultimately require a much less coarse output from the food model than that used at present, i.e. *per capita* consumption averaged for all foodstuffs over each region and an economic model which represents many sectors. However, it does not seem to be intended that the entire model will ultimately be inextricably linked together. Rather, a set of models will be used, possibly at different levels of aggregation, for the analysis of specific global or world regional issues.

The organization of the model in relation to its intended users is one of the most noteworthy features of the project. One of the major criticisms of the MIT model was its deterministic nature. Relationships within the model were fixed in such a way that 'policies' were predetermined at the outset of each computer run. Thus insufficient account was taken of policy responses and of public values and societal structures adapting to fit new conditions. Of course, such matters are very difficult to incorporate into a formal model for reasons we will explain later.

The method chosen by the Mesarovic-Pestel group to circumvent this problem is to use the 'hierarchical decision stratum' approach developed by Mesarovic (Mesarovic, 1970). The logic behind the method is best described by the following two extracts:

A major concern in the application of the computer model is its proper utilization so as to avoid dependence on the deterministic aspects of model operation. In order to avoid this, an interactive method of computer simulation analysis has been developed. The method represents a symbiosis of man and computer in which the computer provides the logical and numerical capability while man provides the values, intuition and experience. The method utilizes an option specification and selection programme which enables the policy analyst or decision-maker to evaluate alternative options on various levels of the decision process, i.e. with respect to goals, strategies, tactical and implementational factors. Special attention is paid to the norm changing processes. (Mesarovic, 1973b.)

In order to be able to deal with the complex of factors involved in the problematique in a way which is sound, credible and systematic, a hierarchical structure has been adopted for the model in which each level in the hierarchy represents the evolution of the world system within a context defined by given a set of laws and principles. Specifically, the levels involved are geo-physical, ecological, technological (man-made energy and mass transfers), economic, institutional, socio-political, value-cultural and human-biological. Such an approach enables the optimal use of confirmed scientific knowledge and available data. (Mesarovic, 1973b.)

Diagrammatically, the separation of functions between the mathematical computer model and the model controller in the hierarchical systems structure is shown in Figure 2. The content of the strata and their relation to different subsystems of the model are indicated by the labels in the diagram.

Who is to provide the endogenous values and policy choices not included in the formal part of the model and how will this inclusion be organized? Several hundred pieces of information representing policy decisions will be required to initiate a typical run of the model and additional pieces will be needed to steer it into a chosen 'future'. Ultimately, it is intended that this information will be provided by policy makers and politicians from each of the regions represented in the model. To preserve confidentiality about some of the other factors in the 'causal' (i.e. non-value laden) part of the model, such as resource stocks and reserves, it is intended that separate sub-models will be located in each region considered in the model and controlled by local high-level policy makers, with external information about the situation in other regions provided by a satellite communication link between control centres. A detailed account of the underlying philosophy of this kind of approach has been supplied by Utsumi (1973) who has advocated a set of satellite linked computer models between the USA and Japan. He considers that, without the participation of

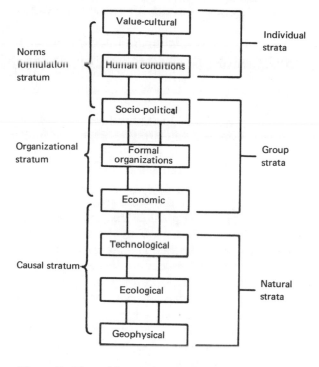

Figure 2. The   Mesarovic–Pestel   model   (from Mesarovic, 1972)

individual countries, national models with the required internal validity cannot be constructed. This approach is similar to that of the LINK model developed by Klein and others (Hickman and coworkers, 1970), some of whom are collaborators on the Mesarovic–Pestel project.

According to Mesarovic (1973b):

The model has been developed up to the stage where it can be used for policy analysis related to a number of critical issues, such as energy resources utilization and technology assessments; food demand and production; population and growth and the effect of timing of birth control programmes; reduction of inequities in regional economic developments; depletion dynamics of certain resources, particularly oil reserves; phosphorus use as fertilizer; regional unemployment; constraints on growth due to labour, energy or export limitation, etc.

In mid–1974, a book describing the work, entitled *Mankind at the Turning Point*, was published (Mesavoric and coworkers, 1974). This concludes, 'All our computer simulations have shown quite clearly that this [the development of a truly global context for decision making] is the only sensible and feasible approach to avoid major regional and ultimately global catastrophe ... clearly the only alternatives are division and conflict,hate and destruction.

THE JAPANESE CLUB OF ROME—A MODEL OF
PRODUCTION REALLOCATION IN THE FUTURE WORLD

The Japanese Club of Rome have set up an extensive programme of research into long-term global futures. Its aim is rather more specific than that of the strategy for survival model. The studies are funded by MITI (Ministry for International Trade and Industry) and emphasis is given to general problems of Third World development, to the situation and role of Japan in the future and to the relationships between the industrialized and the developing nations of the world. The Japanese group are undertaking a range of studies using modelling and other approaches (Kaya and coworkers, 1973a, 1973b); they feel that the most useful results can be achieved if modelling is combined with qualitative and static analytic methods.

The world model being constructed by the group is concerned with the exploration of the effects of various possible distributions of industrial activity between groups of nations, with a view to determining that which is most favourable to the developing countries. The group consider (Kaya and Suzuki, 1974) that the greatest constraint on development in these countries lies in the difficulty of securing markets for their products, and that the developed nations could, as a form of aid, deliberately restrict domestic production of certain products in order to create such markets. The aim of the project is to determine which industrial sectors could, if largely transferred to the developing countries, do most to assist their development, taking into account the respective human and natural resources of each region.

The model contains an optimizing routine which minimizes a 'cost function' which is composed of four factors. The two most important of these refer to total production within each region and global differences in supply and demand within each sector. When the optimizing routine is in operation, the former ('production-gap factor') has the effect of raising the industrial output of regions with low gross regional product, i.e. it tends to reduce international inequalities; the latter ('supply–demand imbalance factor') is included as a basic requirement for economic realism, tending to ensure equality between supply and demand. The other factors in the objective function are added as required for particular studies and comparisons; these are a self-sufficiency factor which places a constraint on trade, and an energy pollution factor which relates pollution to energy consumption. Investment is used as the control variable.

The model contains six industrial sectors: agriculture, mining, light manufacturing, heavy manufacturing, assembly (knowledge-intensive) manufacturing and services. Nine regions are used which are similar to those employed in the Mesarovic–Pestel model; the major difference is that the Middle East and North Africa are absorbed into other regions. For each region industrial production, industrial demand and population are included.

Runs have been carried out giving, in turn, greater weight to the production-gap and supply–demand imbalance factors in the objective function. As might

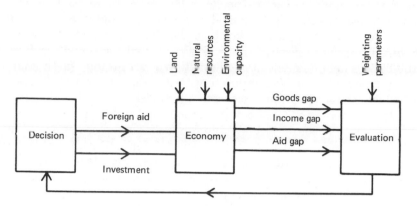

Figure 3. The Japanese Club of Rome model (from Kaya and coworkers, 1973a)

be expected, the former gives a decelerating growth rate in developed countries and accelerates that in developing countries; this is brought about by an increase in the proportion of gross regional product due to agriculture at the expense of light manufacturing in North America, with the reverse situation in Asia. This result arises from the assumption that diminishing returns on investment in agriculture set in more rapidly in Asia, and is dependent to some extent on assumed rates of progress in agricultural technology.

In some versions of the model, aid is used in addition to investment as a control variable. Figure 3 illustrates the optimizing and control processes.

The Japanese group are carrying out several other projects related to the above modelling exercise. They have constructed a model which, instead of treating regions separately, employs a continuous description in terms of levels of development (indicated by GNP *per capita*), the object being to find the solution to an equation describing the development of a time dependent spectrum of world development. In parallel to the computer modelling exercises, studies of mineral resources, technological capability and related factors are being carried out. Further, the Japanese group are attempting to construct a value systems model based on social survey and other data to explain the influence of value changes on people's activity in society (Saito, 1973), which may be incorporated formally into the main body of the global model or simply used as an accessory device providing indirect inputs to that model. There is some contrast here between the Japanese approach and that adopted by the Mesarovic–Pestel and the Bariloche teams (the model of the latter group is discussed below).

With regard to influencing policy, the Japanese again differ from the Mesarovic–Pestel group. Being largely funded by MITI, the team has a closer formal link with a government body; in addition, the group have set up a study committee to look at the detailed policy measures needed to avoid World 3 type catastrophes.

Further, as noted earlier, particular attention is being paid to Japan's situation with respect to potential global scenarios and a complementary project 'Design of the future of Japan in the changing world', is under way (Ishitani, 1973). The object of the project is to find the optimal policies of Japan under both domestic and international constraints, given that the future of Japan is inexorably interlinked with the rest of the world. The project involves the interaction of three separate sub-models: a world model provides inputs to an econometric long-term dynamic model of Japan, in which investment is treated as a control variable whose value is determined by an optimization routine incorporated in a static model of Japan. Investment policy is determined by minimizing the trade balance and the demand-supply gap, subject to constraints imposed domestically (from the long-term Japan model) and from abroad (from the world model).

THE FUNDACION BARILOCHE ALTERNATIVE WORLD MODEL

A Latin American team, working mainly at Fundacion Bariloche in the Argentine, are constructing a world model which they regard as an 'alternative' to World 3 in that the world future is considered from the point of view of developing countries. The team, which is led by A. Herrera, believe that solutions to the Malthusian hypothesis such as those posed in *The Limits to Growth* are conditioned by socio-economic and political contexts. They see the obstacles to an equilibrated development of mankind not as shortages of materials, but as socio-political, at least for the foreseeable future. In order to demonstrate global physical and economic possibilities in the absence of social constraints, they have developed a computer model with the built-in goal of an equitable world society. This model is, therefore, intended to have a quite different role from the Mesarovic–Pestel work, which is designed more or less as a 'general purpose' world planning tool intended to be of use in examining and resolving a fair range of global issues. The Bariloche work has a far more specific purpose. It is primarily concerned with questions of the social and economic development of the less well-off regions of the world, and especially with the Latin American nations.

At one level, the Bariloche model may be viewed as the Third World's antagonistic reaction to *The Limits to Growth*. At an early presentation of the latter at a Club of Rome meeting in Rio de Janeiro, it was decided that such a response was necessary. The Bariloche team point out (Herrera, 1973) that most industrialized countries tend to see world problems as deriving from growth of the world population, especially in developing countries. They believe that, while control of population, pollution and the rational use of resources are essential, they are only complementary to other more fundamental changes required if the major world problems are to be challenged successfully. This was a view strongly reinforced by Third World delegates at the 1974 United Nations World Population Conference. Herrera believes that the central values of the 'western way of life' are not questioned in *The Limits to*

Growth and that, within this western dominated world, its prophesies hold out little hope for poor countries ever enjoying the levels of life realized even today by advanced countries. Thus the Bariloche team reject the solutions proposed in *The Limits to Growth* and remark that their refutation of the MIT work is made in a similar spirit to Marx's refutation of Malthus, which sprang not so much from a different appreciation of 'reality' but from a different conception of the forces determining mankind's destiny.

Thus the Latin American model is not presented as being a 'general purpose' model. Nevertheless, within its own value structure, it may be as general in its view of the world as the Mesarovic–Pestel model is to a western oriented view of the world. More simply, the model may be seen as built around a different philosophy.

Even though the underlying philosophy of the Bariloche and Mesarovic–Pestel models differs, their formal structures are certainly not totally dissimilar. Indeed, very many of the underlying assumptions, parameters and structural relationships are alike. What is different in the Bariloche study is the *emphasis* placed on the importance of each sector, the rules for determining the possible future world development portrayed by the model (e.g. investment allocation to different sectors) and the interpretation placed on the model results. (This last point was poorly appreciated by the MIT group, the impression given being of a certain air of finality and definitiveness with regard to the numerical results obtained.) For example, in the Bariloche model, in each of the geographic blocs there are sectors representing the economy, population, health, food, education, non-renewable resources, energy and pollution. Details of international trade are not considered, except that an overall long-term payments balance is assumed. The economic sector contains five productive sectors—food, housing services, educational services, other consumption goods and services, and capital goods; and two production factors—capital and labour. Like the Mesarovic–Pestel model, production levels for each sector are based on a Cobb–Douglas type production function. The central feature of the model is a 'function of basic needs' which determines the amount of material and cultural goods a human being needs for his 'full development' without wasting resources. It is computed by dividing the levels of physical production of food, housing, health and teaching services by the population. Once the adequate levels of this function have been reached, it is assumed that any economic surplus will be allocated in a 'free society'. The model contains an 'optimizing' or 'search' routine which is used to determine the mix of allocations which would cause a goal function described in terms of basic needs to be achieved in the shortest possible time. Since so many of the basic needs appear to determine life expectancy, the routine is used to determine the strategy which raises average life expectancy at birth most rapidly.

Thus the model has been built to examine:

(a) the possibility of reaching certain levels of satisfaction of basic needs in terms of physical consumption *per capita*;

that 'the lack of an adequate and stable institutional basis has imposed serious restrictions on progress, particularly with respect to the need to attract cooperation—from both within Holland and internationally—of suitable persons and groups of the high expertise and broad viewpoint needed for these problems'. For this reason the group has decided to concentrate on problems of food supply and distribution. Although not explicitly stated, personnel problems also seem to have been experienced by other groups.

In the Battelle research programme entitled DEMATEL (Decision Making Trial and Evaluation Laboratory), the Institute is investigating the development of decision making techniques for the 'amelioration of problems of world-wide concern' (Thiemann, 1973a). As part of the DEMATEL programme, the identification of world problems (to be discussed in Chapter 3) is taking place in Geneva, while at Richland, USA, groups are developing a world model. Their first attempt, GLOBE 5, was based on a flow chart for Forrester's World 2, except that pollution was internally controlled. A development into GLOBE 6 came next, which seems to be roughly the same as GLOBE 5, except that it is divided into rich/poor regions and is implemented interactively.

More specifically, World 2 and GLOBE 6 contain the same basic variables (population, agriculture, industry, resources and pollution), the latter model incorporating them for each of the two regions. The major differences have been described by Burnett and Dionne (1973).

The UK Department of the Environment is undertaking several modelling activities, including the construction of exploratory world models. The motives for this work, and some details of it, have been described by the (then) Chief Government Scientist, Sir Alan Cottrell (1973). Cottrell and several of his colleagues were convinced of the importance of the issues raised by the MIT team and of dynamic modelling as an appropriate means of studying them. As suggested by the quote from Tinker in chapter 1 his view was more favourable to the MIT work than that of many colleagues in the Government's scientific staff; however, it is clear that dynamic modelling work was considered worthwhile and it was decided that a world model would be constructed in an attempt to improve on those of MIT. The model is expected to be useful in testing, in an experimental way, the future effects of certain policy options, but it is not clear to what extent it will be used as a policy making aid.

This world model is based on fairly well used ideas in economic theory, but contains some novel features. The world is divided into three economic regions—poor, middle and rich—each of which is composed of a number of sectors. Total investment for each region is determined from a set of utility curves and this sum is allocated between sectors by extrapolating past trends for each sector to estimate its future profitability as based on a continuation of past investment patterns. A particular feature of interest in the model is the illustration of the substitution of one energy source by another as production costs of the former rise, e.g. because of the necessity of mining lower-grade ores, and the possibly severe consequences that could result from a delay in implementing the necessary shifts in investment. This problem has previously been considered in a smaller DOE model (Roberts, 1973).

In many respects, the model is similar to those described previously, such as in the use of Cobb–Douglas production functions and the assumption of exponential increases in productivity in some economic sectors. Forecasts of technical progress are very uncertain and they constitute one of the most difficult aspects of building a world model. Very few positive statements can be made; however, the DOE have recognized and incorporated the existence of upper limits to efficiency in certain areas, such as for power stations and in photosynthesis. It is understood that certain data to be used to calibrate the model is confidential at present, but it may be that more complete publication will be possible in due course.

In the United States, the Environmental Protection Agency is using a series of models to examine regional resource allocation and pollution hazards (House, 1973). This work has a similar but rather less extensive function to that carried out in the UK Department of the Environment. In California, Watt and coworkers (1973) are building global models with particular attention to long-term climatic problems. In Czechoslovakia, Zeman (1973) is using a large-scale model to examine 'pessimal' forecasts (i.e. those affected by potentially dangerous constraints).

Other researchers such as Krauch (1973) in Germany and Dator (1972) in Hawaii have experimented with the use of global models as a discussion tool in a public forum, including 'experts' and lay discussants. Some experiments use a 'phone-in' facility to a television studio.

Many other groups have shown an interest in world modelling and have constructed experimental models. Seminars have been held in both Western, Eastern and Third World countries. Many groups concerned with world problems have used models to explore particular aspects of those issues and their interrelations. Others have built laboratory models to examine the possibilities and limitations of large-scale models.

The Science Policy Research Unit and the authors have been intimately concerned in both kinds of study: the STAFF (Social and Technological Alternatives for the Future) programme is an ongoing research activity into world problems, particularly those related to underdevelopment. A group has also carried out a detailed feasibility study into the possibilities of building 'socio-economic' models for Europe (Clark and coworkers, 1973 and 1974), and some of the findings from this study are discussed later. We have not discussed these studies in detail here, nor several others which we consider to be important, since they will be referred to where appropriate in other parts of the book.

With this brief description of the second generation of world models, their origins and their differences, we are in a position to discuss their theoretical and social legitimacy, i.e. how well the models themselves may be considered to represent the 'real world' and how acceptable and useful they may be as aids to social policy.

3

Systems and World Problems

'PROBLEM: WHAT IS A PROBLEM?'

Nordbeck (1971) has attempted to answer this question using 16 available definitions of 'problem' as source material. He concludes that 'A problem or a problem situation exists when one experiences a need or demand to achieve— through some kind of activity or search—from a certain existing situation, another imagined situation, a goal situation, which cannot be attained either immediately or by any automatic, habitual activity'.

There is, of course, no objective criterion to determine the existence of a 'problem'. A problem exists if a situation is thought to be undesirable and purposive action is required to ameliorate it. In one society, a problem situation may exist at a particular time while, in another society or at another time, the same situation may not be considered to be undesirable. The changing views within a society are vividly illustrated by Art Buchwald who, in a syndicated column under the title 'Miss Pollution the Winner', considers how, in the past, Miss Crime in the Streets, Miss Wars, Miss Hunger, Miss Poverty, and Miss Desegregation have each been voted as 'Miss Problem of the Year' in the United States; at the end of their reign they pass out of fashion and, like Miss World, no longer receive attention.

Quite apart from fashion, however, the importance of the cultural setting for the perception of problems has been widely discussed. One society may describe problems to an ideologically different society which the latter does not recognize. For example, some cultures have considered that, under certain circumstances, suicide is acceptable and even desirable, whereas modern Western civilizations clearly do not take this view.

One does not have to go very far, however, to obtain a wide consensus of agreement on the undesirability of a large number of situations, and it is such situations which will be considered in this book.

Further discussion of when a problem is a 'world' problem, and hence a candidate for inclusion in a world model, is required since, historically, no situation generally accepted as undesirable has affected everybody. Indeed, there are very few potential problem situations which are truly worldwide in character—a nuclear holocaust and severe atmospheric pollution could perhaps come into this category. Problems of a more local character must therefore be considered as 'world problems' also, provided that the situations are regarded as serious by the people concerned and that their incidence is widespread, both in space and time.

Several attempts have been made to list and categorize world problems. Two of the most ambitious have been carried out by the Union of International Associations in Brussels and Battelle Memorial Institute in Geneva. The UIA contest strongly that problems should not be considered in isolation and point out that, frequently, groups have independently studied related problems, leading to much duplication of research effort. An objective of their work is therefore to clarify relationships between problems and the way they are nested within one another.

By scanning journals and reference books and consulting United Nations agencies, a list of problems, with associated information, was drawn up. Each entry has been sent to specialists for verification and amendment of information regarding, among other things, the incidence of the problems, possible remedies and subsidiary and associated problems. To date, about 3,000 problems have been listed, ranging from 'poverty' to 'unification of churches' and 'plunder of Eastern art treasures', and it is envisaged that the final listing will contain up to 5,000 entries (Lowe, 1972).

The UIA have explored several possible classifications of world problems, one being the following:

Physical violence and conflict problems.
Physical sustenance problems.
Natural environment problems.
Psycho-social problems.
Strategy, policy, decision-making and action problems.
Interdisciplinary, transdisciplinary and cross-modal problems.

Another classification scheme suggested by UIA, with reference to the organizational structure required for the solution of problems, is along the dimension of simplicity/complexity, as follows:

Docile isolated problems (relatively independent of other problems and contained within an organized and orderly environment; comparatively easy to attack).

Docile problem groups (the solution to one problem may worsen others in the group; the organization needs an overall strategy).

Dynamic interactive problems (changes in one problem area give rise to changes in another; an organization cannot act without taking into account other organizations).

Aggressive interactive problems (interactive problems whose behaviour is not understood, requiring a very high level of cooperation between organizations).

World models are mainly concerned with 'physical sustenance' and 'natural environment' problems, considered as 'dynamically interactive' and of an international scale. 'Conflict' problems have been approached by 'gaming' representations. We will see later (Chapter 4) that 'social' problems are difficult to account for in computer simulation and we will argue that the question of policy implementation and organizational structure has not been considered sufficiently by modellers.

Finally, a hierarchical structure reflecting the ease with which problems are perceived by different organizations and individuals is presented by UIA.

Level 1: direct consequence of lack of economic resources, e.g. malnutrition, disease, rich–poor gap.
Level 2: social consequences of level 1 problems, e.g. refugees, illiteracy, crime.
Level 3: consequences of adaptation to environment containing levels 1 and 2 problems, e.g. population explosion, urban decay, mental health.
Level 4: organizational or societal coordination or resource-allocation problems, arising from the institutionalization of organizational response to past low-level problems, which prevent adequate response to current problems, e.g. selection of high-priority projects, design of adequate systems, problems of relevance.
Level 5: conceptual, psychological and cultural problems arising from lack of communication associated with level 4 problems, making justification by decision makers of interterritorial, interdisciplinary or interjurisdictional solutions difficult, e.g. problems of meaning of the same terms in different cultures or disciplines.
Level 6: conceptual and cultural problems opposing the provision of a framework for the solution of level 5 problems.
Level 7: lack of feedback sensitivity of organizations, disciplines and individuals.

Levels 1–3 are generally recognized within governmental programmes, level 4 by those studying planning and decision-making and levels 5–7 only in isolated studies and crisis analysis.

The UIA intend to use their work as follows: to publish a 'Yearbook of world problems', to produce 'problem maps' to show how problems are interlinked, to use computer interactive graphics as a device to handle problem networks, and as a permanent data base for research and policy purposes.

A listing of perceived world problems is undoubtedly of value since it provides researchers with a perspective for their work and may lead to an establishment of the goals of society. While structuring is clearly arbitrary to some extent—'one man's grouping tends to be another's straightjacket' (Lowe, 1972)—it is necessary to obtain some insight into the nature of problems and to put them into a context. The form of the structure can be different for different purposes; problems can, for example, be grouped according to a hierarchical structure, showing how some problems are derived from, or are 'special cases' of 'primary' problems, according to a taxonomy derived from 'conventional' usage, which is usually based on academic disciplines, or according to the 'scale' of the problem (local, national, international) which determines the kind of policy-making body required to effect a solution. A combination of these schemes can, of course, be used to form a structure.

The last categorization of the UIA is clearly reminiscent of the Mesarovic-Pestel modelling approach. The idea of regarding human systems as an interlinked hierarchy, where problems developing at a given level could affect other levels, was used in the information control system constructed by Beer in his cybernetic 'Chile' model (Beer, 1972 and 1973; Adams, 1973).

As part of their DEMATEL project, the Battelle Memorial Institute in Geneva is searching for a pattern of objectives of contemporary societies. To help achieve this aim, the Institute has, by analysing the texts of reports and speeches, obtained 60 topics considered by various influential individuals and organizations as critical issues of worldwide concern. These have been distilled into 48 classified problems, on the basis of which a questionnaire has been developed and sent to a large number of cultural, political, economic and scientific leaders of the world. The chief purpose of the questionnaire is to ascertain how interrelationships between the 48 problems are perceived; to this end an interaction matrix is being compiled.

In their proposal for the establishment of 'Councils of urgent studies', Cellarius and Platt (1972) have compiled a list of problems, classified into six broad disciplinary groups (physical technology and engineering (crisis related), biotechnology, behaviour and personal relations, national social structures, world structure, channels of effectiveness) and 25 narrower areas. They suggest that, at present, one-third of the fields they categorize are badly neglected, particularly problems related to organizations, mass communications, politics, large-scale change, peace-keeping structure, developing countries, political and economic support of urgent research, and systems analysis. Some other attempts to list and classify world problems are briefly discussed in an article in *Futures* (5, 5, 1973, pp. 516–518).

An attempt to establish the linkages between problems, or groups of problems, provides a valuable guide for the integration of research efforts in different fields and for the possible development of world models. 'Cross-impact' techniques have been developed to put perceived linkages on a quantitative basis.

Our effort is largely directed towards establishing the efficacy of a particular group of techniques, i.e. quantitative dynamic analysis, which may be applicable to some fields but not to others, and for this purpose a broad categorization of problems into the following three groups seems to be useful:

(a) 'Shortage' problems: e.g. of food, energy and resources.
(b) 'Environmental' problems: e.g. pollution, soil erosion.
(c) 'Social' problems: e.g. health, population, crime, ideological and international conflict.

(a) and (b) are to a considerable extent physical, technological and ecological problems, while (c) is concerned with the structure of society. As with every classification scheme, however, the distinctions are far from perfect; undernourishment, for example, can be considered in terms of the 'technological' problem of artificially increasing land productivity, as a problem arising from social inequality and maldistribution of food, or as a 'derived' problem caused by overpopulation. Nevertheless, the scheme is useful for our purposes and we shall later apply it in discussing the relevance of quantitative techniques used in the physical, biological and social sciences in the analysis of world problems.

The above classification indirectly includes problems of a moral nature. However, these issues are very nebulous and so far do not qualify as 'problems' in world modelling terms. They have not been considered in any world models to date, except in the interpretation of results. Indeed, as we have seen, the early world models associated with the Club of Rome included only a very restricted range of issues; those of more recent origin incorporate different sets of issues, but none outside those covered above.

For many people, the most important problems are those of a personal nature. These often involve relationships with others and again we have not included such questions in our classification, the reason in this case being that no policy changes can directly hope to eliminate them. It is very doubtful whether dynamic analysis, or any other form of analytic or forecasting technique, can be of value. No society has been able to eradicate unhappiness. Freud has given three factors which ensure that man can never be perfectly happy and secure: the decay and death of the body, the impossibility of removing the threat of natural disasters and the behaviour of individuals as leaving something to be desired in their interactions with others. These problems are concerned with the nature of man and the inherent features of his existence; if 'solutions' of any kind exist they are essentially theological and quite outside our realm of discussion.

Thus the problems we are considering are those at a societal level rather than those at the level of the individual. The solution of these problems would not transform the world into a paradise, but few would deny their overwhelming importance in providing freedom from deprivation and fear and in giving individuals a reasonable environment in which to live. The application of dynamic analysis to them, as in the world models, seems eminently justified if it helps to give an understanding and points towards solutions. In this and the following chapter, an examination is made of the potential and the limitations of the technique of dynamic analysis when directed towards these ends.

THE CONTRIBUTION OF SYSTEMS THINKING

Most of those issues which are considered to be 'world problems' are the concern not of a single discipline, but of a 'hybrid' of the physical, biological and social sciences and their mutual interrelationships. Consequently, for these issues, the concept of 'systems thinking', that is, taking account of several factors simultaneously, becomes especially appealing.

By definition, a *system* is merely a set of at least two interconnected elements, such that each element is related to all other elements, either directly or indirectly (Ackoff, 1971). Generally, the concept of 'holism' is implicit in the idea of a system; the elements are viewed as forming a complex or unitary whole (Kast and Rosenzweig, 1970).

Most of the ideas and concepts found to be of value in helping us understand events in the real world have come from individuals working in particular fields. The separation of areas of learning into academic disciplines has clearly been fruitful; as insight has increased, progress has often necessitated that individuals can only contribute by becoming specialists. As they have developed, disciplines have tended to acquire their own features and techniques and to be represented by a 'peer group' of professional researchers. (We will discuss this concept in detail later.)

While it is beyond dispute that 'partialism' (i.e. the process of attempting to separate and explain phenomena by going to an increasing level of detail and specialization) has been useful, the point at issue is to what extent a holistic approach can be of value. It is clear that many systems, whose evolution depends essentially on the interactions between its components, demand a holistic approach. Most of our world problems fall into this category. Even for world problem areas, however, the separation of issues is often beneficial. It is useful to identify particular pollutants, particular technologies and particular social institutions. Both separation of issues and the resulting specialization within disciplines are essential parts of the creation of knowledge necessary for their study. This is a consequence of the need to simplify in order to comprehend. But the reintegration of these issues is also required. Particular issues, or even particular parameters, once understood, are included back into the comprehensive theory. In the reintegration, reduction of many parameters into a few is the process whereby the whole can be comprehended.

The problem is clearly to determine the 'optimum' level of description for the purpose at hand. In our view, the MIT models did not give a sufficiently detailed level of description for many of the parameters. The difficulty is that many 'wholes', such as 'pollution', tend to be rather theoretical concepts with a poor empirical base; the statement that the pollution level has a certain value does not mean very much and a variable 'pollution' can only be quantified in an arbitrary way. Some disaggragation into types of pollutant seems essential for meaningful quantification.

Malthus (with whom both Forrester and Meadows found a resonance) and, for that matter, Marx, despite their rather different views on 'details', quite clearly were in favour of holism. Marx is quite explicit that society and nature should be regarded as parts of a single system: 'Natural science will one day incorporate the science of man, just as the science of man will one day incorporate natural science; there will be but a single science' (quoted in Bottomore and Rubel, 1956). Unfortunately, with the continued fragmentation of social and natural sciences in this century, and despite considerable progress in many areas, few people would disagree that this happy state has not yet arrived.

Even so, there is, nowadays, fairly general agreement that, in discussing policy issues, all relevant processes should be accounted for somehow in the 'system', and this is witnessed by current growth of interdisciplinary research.

In considering the various types of systems in our universe, Boulding (1956) provides a classification of systems which sets forth a hierarchy of levels, which have been listed and commented on by Kast and Rosenzweig (1970). They range through physical, botanical, animal, human, social and transcendental systems; the level of greatest relevance to world problems is clearly the social level, or rather the impact of this on the human level although, as explained in the previous section, we are not concerned with the individual human being in isolation; in so far as they have effect (physiological or cultural) on the individual and society, physical and biological systems also need to be considered.

As described in Chapter 1, a recent development in the study of systems is 'general systems theory' which is an attempt to formulate and develop principles which hold for systems in general. The motives for its development have been summarized by a pioneer in the field, von Bertalanffy, who considers that classical science has tended to neglect biological and social problems, and feels that new conceptual tools are needed to deal with these areas (von Bertalanffy, 1969). Ackoff (1960) believes that to overcome these problems, concepts which permit disciplines to be related via a common methodological approach are required. This would, he says, entail theoretical breakthroughs such as a common scale of measurement and educational changes to encourage the right kind of interdisciplinary approach.

Ackoff and von Bertalanffy thus both feel that quantitative systems research cannot be conducted efficiently with the tools at present available, and the concept of a general systems theory is certainly an attractive one. Unless and until it becomes a practical reality, however, systems analysis will have to be carried out using the traditional approaches which are considered in the next section.

APPROACHES TO SYSTEMS ANALYSIS AND MODELLING

According to Watt (1968), systems analysis consists simply in the determination of those elements which are important in a system. And he suggests that systems simulation, systems optimization and systems measurement are other facets of the systems approach. (Cited by Dale, M. B. 'Systems Analysis in Ecology' in *Systems Behaviour* (Beishon, J. and Peters, G., Eds., Open University, 1972). These elements are selectee according to those characteristics of the real world which the investigator deems relevant to the processes he wishes to study. However, it is probably more convenient to consider selection of elements as merely the first phase of systems analysis; this process continues with the development of relationships between the elements, investigation of their consequences and the testing of the structure obtained.

In order to maintain both comprehension and manageability in the analysis of a system, some kind of model, i.e. a simplified or idealized representation, is essential. Following Ackoff (1962), a *model* can be defined as an idealized representation of reality describing some phenomenon whose behaviour is to be highlighted. This definition immediately brings out the issue of the necessary simplification incurred in building a model and of the purposive nature of any model in the conscious choice of phenomena to be highlighted.

Numerous taxonomies of models have been proposed and it is clear from the literature that the word 'model' is used in many different ways; the observation of Hoos (1972) that 'the word 'model' is second only to 'system' in ambiguity of meaning and ubiquity of usage' seems very apt. One simple and well known classification (e.g. Chorley and Haggett, 1967) divides models into the categories of iconic, analogue, symbolic and mental. Iconic models are those in which properties of the real world are represented with only a change of scale, such as a model aircraft constructed for wind-tunnel testing. Analogue models are similarly 'physical' constructions, but real-world properties are represented by different properties. An example is a map where political regions are differentiated by the use of colour. Symbolic and mental models, in terms of which world problems are analysed and to which our use of the word 'model' will in future be confined, are concerned with formal assertions made in logical terms, these assertions being made in verbal terms, in the case of mental models, and in mathematical terms in the case of symbolic models. We are, of course, most concerned with the latter, and particularly with those methods of systems analysis in which a computer is used as an aid to construction.

In many areas, quantitative techniques are, in principle, applicable, but, for an adequate description, the system of equations obtained is too complex to be solved analytically. It is these areas which are often best described by simulation models, which use the ability of a computer to handle a large number of variables simultaneously and perform repetitive mathematical operations quickly.

However, mathematical techniques and computers have their limitations, especially in that they involve further approximation. Many scientists, particularly those in the social sciences, feel that, even with the aid of computers, quantitative models are too rigid and can never represent all the complexities of reality. Mathematical models are, for many practical purposes, complementary to mental models, although often the two methods are regarded as being in competition; from the purely scientific point of view, there seems to be no way of resolving the dispute about the correct balance, except on 'pragmatic' grounds, i.e. by assessing the value of models in practice. For this reason, we will consider many case studies of the use of models in Chapter 6.

Another dimension along which we can classify possible approaches to modelling, besides that concerning the degree of mathematical representation, is the 'philosophical' one whose extremes can be labelled 'rationalism' and 'empiricism' (Mitroff and Turoff, 1973). In a 'rationalist' model the emphasis is on the justification of a representation independently of empirical considerations, i.e. the truth of a model depends on its formal theoretical content, rather than on any data input. The 'empirical' approach is based on the assumption that what can be known about a system depends entirely on its empirical content and not on the prior assumption of any theory. Thus, data is that which is prior to and justifies theory, not the other way round.

In practice, it is not possible to realize 'pure' forms of either of these categories: a theory must depend ultimately on perceptions of the real world; data is inevitably conditioned to some extent by the way one chooses to look at the world. The technique of Forrester and Meadows comes rather close to 'rationalism', which is justified if theory is at a sufficiently advanced stage of development. Trend extrapolation and statistical techniques are essentially empirical procedures and are useful mainly for short-term projections, where it can be assumed that underlying mechanisms will be invarient in the timespan of interest, so that these mechanisms need not be examined nor possible changes in them postulated.

Mitroff and Turoff (1973) label these approaches 'Leibnizian' and 'Lockean', respectively, and discuss compromises between them. In these theory and data are generally regarded as inseparable. In the 'Kantian' method, at least two theoretical representations are used, and data is collected, from which it is hoped that the 'best' representation of the problem can be selected. This was essentially the method used in a recent feasibility study undertaken by the Science Policy Research Unit (Clark and coworkers, 1974). The aim was to examine the possibility of constructing a socio-economic model of Europe to include a number of social, economic and demographic factors. In view of the current uncertainty surrounding economic and social theory, a number of models were constructed and independently analysed.

Another compromise is the 'Hegelian' method; it is here assumed that, on any issue, a plan and a diametrically opposed counterplan can be constructed and the 'true' nature of a system is revealed through a debate which leads to synthesis or reconciliation of the opposing conceptions. These conceptions are Leibnizian (theoretical) representations which, in the debate, are applied to the same Lockean data set; the purpose is to reveal the underlying assumptions behind the representations by showing how the data must be interpreted to support them. This approach is used principally for poorly defined systems and is applied in structured discussions.

Finally, the 'Singerian–Churchmanian' method is essentially a pragmatic approach and is explicitly goal-oriented: every description of the present is assumed to be based on some normative conception of the future. This is the most difficult to apply using mathematical models and corresponds most closely to the 'incremental' method used in practical policy making.

In this book we are primarily concerned with dynamic representations. The world problems considered earlier change through time and dynamic analysis permits the explicit representation of time-dependent processes. Further, dynamic modelling takes account of the displacement in time between 'cause' and 'effect' at any given level of representation. These time delays can affect the stability of a process. For example, in World 3, delays are considered to be responsible for the various collapses. Empirically, it is observed that the impact of legislation, or of economic or climatic disturbances, is delayed and that repercussions affect different parts of the processes involved at different times. In some circumstances cycles, or oscillations, are observed and often it may be postulated that these arise through the influence of such delays. Dynamic models, therefore, offer one method of gaining understanding of these processes and of anticipating their effects.

THE ROLE OF MODELS IN FORECASTING

We have discussed, in broad terms, some approaches to the modelling of world problems and have described in some detail the efforts which are now under way to construct global computer models. At this point it is necessary to clarify what we see to be the role of modelling, particularly in the context of a forecasting exercise.

Following Hesse (1966), 'a model may be considered as a factual description if it represents a positive analogy to the real-world situation in all aspects previously tested, and if it has surplus content which in principle is capable of test'. This definition stresses 'surplus content' in that a model should be capable of showing behaviour which can also occur in the real world, although the real world may not yet have done so. The inclusion of surplus content in a dynamic model provides the capability of working with an accelerated time basis without waiting for the real world to evolve such behaviour; it thus opens up the possibility of 'forecasting'.

Forecasting and planning are clearly very closely related and it is difficult to imagine any kind of planning taking place without some sort of forecasting, however implicit this may be. We consider that, in the long run, it is the production of good plans which is important (in the sense that they turn out to be effective with a minimum of deleterious consequences) rather than accurate forecasts *per se*.

'Futures' for the purpose of policy making are normally described as short, medium, and long or 'distant' although what precisely is meant by these terms depends on the area under investigation. Economists, for example, would normally describe a ten-year forecast as 'long term', but this is, of course, brief compared with time horizons considered in the world models. (The world models described in Chapter 2 are largely concerned with possibilities for the next thirty years or so, somewhat less than the hundred-odd years considered with the MIT models.) The 'worth' of information about the future for policy purposes clearly falls off more or less rapidly according to the purposes for which it is required. Thus information about long-term trends is quite likely to be of little value for short-term investment decisions. It is mainly for this reason that, to date, relatively little effort has been expended on long-term forecasting. R and D investments, however, are realized on a longer time scale and, as the magnitude of expenditure increases, so does the need for satisfactory medium- and long-term projections.

While short-term forecasts can often be adequately based on fairly straight-forward extrapolative techniques, this does not seem sufficient for longer-term projections where a deeper understanding of the mechanisms underlying historical events is needed. In short-term forecasting, decisions are mostly taken in the light of expected, but unchangeable trends. For viewing the long-term future, simple extrapolation (even in the guise of Kahn and Wiener's (1967) 'multi-fold' trend) may not be as appropriate as the dynamic modelling methods discussed in this book.

The use of the term 'forecasting' gives rise to much misunderstanding. It is often used in the sense of 'prediction', meaning the assertion that a particular event will inevitably occur in the future with a high probability. Any dynamic model can be used for prediction, as can less sophisticated methods such as direct curve extrapolation. Forecasting, in a broader sense, means the attempt to foresee the results of various possible actions: if a certain plan is followed, what will be the consequences? It is also used in the prescriptive sense of showing whether or not a given desired future is inconsistent with mechanisms believed to operate in the real world and what actions are required to make the occurrence of that future more likely. The spirit of this last description of forecasting seems to be the most commonly accepted among long-range forecasters and is contained to a greater or lesser degree in all the world modelling activities so far described. However, such a definition still leaves much room for disagreement and mutual criticism, especially when there is little consensus as to the true nature of constraints and mechanisms, which is often the situation with world problems.

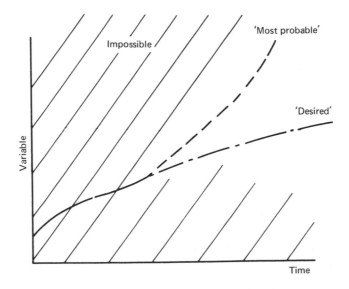

Figure 5. Possible, probable and desired futures

In a particular exercise, in the light of the mechanisms assumed to operate, it may turn out that the most probable future is, for example, a continuation of historical trend as shown in Figure 5. That this is the most probable trend does not, however, exclude a wide range of other trends bounded by regions of 'impossible futures'. A change in the trend might result from a particular decision to 'steer' towards a desired goal. The boundaries assumed for the choices of possible futures derive from constraints dictated by, for example, the thermal capacity of the earth (about which there is a matter of great uncertainty and disagreement). The boundaries may not just be considered impenetrable in a physical sense, but more often may be set by prevailing views of socio-political factors (about which there is even greater controversy).

In fact, the range of possible futures is always highly constrained in one way or another, so that, in effect, choices are determined very largely by external factors beyond the control of the policy bodies using the results of the exercise. To this extent, any forecast must be considered 'deterministic' rather than 'normative'.

A Council of Europe Report (1973) provides a concise categorization of approaches to long-range forecasting into projection studies, prospective research and decisional research, which in many ways complements the distinctions we have drawn between different modelling approaches.

The report considers that the three approaches are not entirely unrelated; they are complementary rather than alternative methods of forecasting.

Projection is particularly suitable for detecting problems, difficulties and inconsistencies in apparent trends, by projecting present factors and structures into the future. Prospective research studies the possibility of changing current trends and structures, by speculating about the future. Decisional research explores ways and means of achieving a future objective and optimising decision-making.

In fact, any forecasting exercise is likely to contain an element of each approach. Although it is an oversimplification, it is appropriate to interpret forecasting as comprising three intimately related activities, roughly corresponding to the Council of Europe definitions, as follows:

(a) Projection: This corresponds most closely to the old idea of forecasting as a means of precise prediction. Here the logic of a postulated future is demonstrated through a systematic study of causal mechanisms and by drawing on historical analogy. This activity includes extrapolation of 'present trends' and examination of the consequences of various policy alternatives. Straightforward naive, single variable projection, regression analysis and more recently multiple variable extrapolation using, for example, computer simulation models, are most commonly employed.

(b) Scenario building: This visionary or image creation activity is very important to long-term forecasting. Apart from literary works (including science fiction, moral and political writings), techniques such as Delphi and 'brainstorming' are used in this way.

38

(c) Policy analysis: Here the repercussions and 'trade-offs' of the choices implicit in the other two activities are examined in relation to other areas of public policy. 'Cross impact' studies, Programme Policy Budgeting System and cost benefit analysis have all been used in this way.

The activities are represented schematically in Figure 6, which emphasizes, that, in long-term forecasting especially, there is a very strong link between the 'projection' activity and the 'visionary' activity. Thus, for example, any 'prospective' or 'image building' activity will take due account of projections of variables such as population, and the choice of variables or theory in a projection will involve certain normative assumptions.

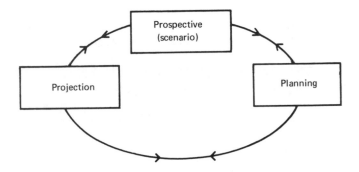

Figure 6. Interacting forecasting activities

As indicated above, systems analytic and other techniques have been developed in an attempt to improve the precision and consistency of all stages of forecasting. However, it is in the 'projection' stage of a forecasting exercise especially that modelling methods are likely to be of most use. (We are including exploration of the effect of alternative policies and contingencies in this definition of projection.)

The implication so far has been that forecasting is the major purpose of model building. Nevertheless, it is probably true that a better forecasting capability is gained, directly or indirectly, from most intellectual activity. Several distinctive potential uses of dynamic models have been advanced and it is useful to review them briefly here.

(1) A precursor to rational forecasting and planning must be an 'explanation' of how the real world behaves. This entails the building up of descriptions about causal processes. 'Explanation' to us means the inference of causal links between phenomena. Associative relationships, such as those derived from statistical estimation, only 'describe' a system, they do not 'explain' it, i.e. do not constitute a demonstration that certain things follow *necessarily* from others. The ability of dynamic models to be used to take explicit account of causal mechanisms, in the form, for example, of time delays, provides advan-

tages over other methods. In many instances, there is little practical opportunity for building a reliable model of a particular situation of interest and, in this case, argument must rest entirely on the basis of general principles formulated from descriptions of analogous situations. By drawing attention to points considered essential to the behaviour of a system, but where data and theory are weak, modelling can act as a springboard for further research and the development of stronger theory. This will be especially important in the 'hybrid' systems characteristic of world problems. Computer models obviously use theories but they should also, themselves, provide further insights into real world behaviour by helping to 'articulate' ideas about the way the world behaves in a new or clearer fashion.

(2) The identification of causal mechanisms is a necessary step in a model designed to aid the control of events. For such a model, the emphasis is on the determination of the values of a set of control or policy variables such that an optimum path is followed when the results are implemented on the real system. For many social processes experimentation is not feasible and understanding may be improved by using a model representation.

(3) A modelling activity may have an 'indirect' value in acting as a useful focus of discussion, particularly for an interdisciplinary team where there is a strong need for various ideas to be put into a context; for example, 'gaming' approaches may be used to observe and stimulate conflict situations. Individual models can also be constructed to illustrate 'viewpoints' of individual team members, an example of the 'Hegelian' approach considered in the previous section. Used in this way, it has been suggested that models have a powerful educative role.

The resolution of world problems requires that policy decisions be made. A model constructed for (2), or for forecasting in the broader sense, is potentially a direct means of deriving such decisions. At a lower level, a model constructed for (1) can assist understanding of the problem in hand and hence provide information which can be helpful to the formation of policy. (3) represents potential values of modelling at a lower level still.

To help us reach conclusions on the utility of global models, it is convenient to divide the kind of modelling activity we have described into three classes according to their style of policy application.

In some circumstances, it is possible that a given model may accommodate the views of the majority of interested parties to a discussion. Such a model may be called a *'policy' model* since it may be used to test some aspects of public policies in a more or less non-controversial manner agreeable to all parties.

In more controversial issues where there is a lack of a common viewpoint, several models may be employed, their use being to assist each party to a debate to understand more fully their own and others' points of view and their consequences. These may be called *'viewpoint' models* and most models used in policy fall into this class.

Finally, there are *'experimental' models* which contribute in an indirect manner to the least well understood policy issues. These help to establish general views and suggest broad strategies for dealing with issues.

We will argue in Chapter 6 that relatively few models qualify as 'policy' models and that, at the present state-of-the-art, the value of most, models in public policy is largely limited to the 'viewpoint' and 'experimental' categories.

4

The Theoretical Foundations

World modelling is a comparatively new form of research activity; but it depends for its success largely on the ability of researchers to learn from, and make use of, ideas and methods developed in other fields over many decades. The characteristics of these fields, and the relationship of world modelling to them with respect to both 'academic' and 'institutional' considerations, comprises the discussion in this chapter.

THE EVOLUTION OF KNOWLEDGE—PARADIGMS

To a great extent, the evolution of knowledge has consisted of the construction and testing of theories and models of various kinds. A theory consists in a set of axioms or postulates, whose truth is taken for granted, and theorems, logically derived from them, which are true if the postulates are. Theories are usually thought to be derived from observation and induction, the latter, following Popper (1963), being 'the inferring of universal laws from particular observed instances'. Systems analysis, or modelling, however, rarely involves the inference of universal laws; rather, models are usually formed from theories combined with phenomenological evidence to produce as 'holistic' a representation of a *particular* system as is deemed necessary for description, prediction or control of events and processes.

Models and theories are used as a means of coordinating the wide variety of sense impressions we receive. However, a view now commanding wide acceptance is that a 'paradigm'—a general theory or structural framework—is necessary for perception itself and that understanding can only be achieved within the context of a particular paradigm. This implies that observations are determined by a preconceived theoretical framework, as well as, or instead of, the other way round.

Kuhn (1962) suggests that the development of science consists of the following. A paradigm is set up, and scientists then develop this conceptual framework and use it to solve 'puzzles' which are themselves suggested by the framework. This period of 'normal science' ends when a considerable amount of evidence has been accumulated to indicate that some 'puzzles' cannot be solved within the framework; a 'scientific revolution' then occurs, a new, more general framework being set up, which, being considered by a consensus of scientists as being more valid, constitutes a new paradigm, within which normal science is once more carried out. Kuhn considers that what we see depends both upon what we look at and also upon what previous experience has taught us to see; what are perceived as scientific problems, and whether solutions are possible, depends on the paradigm of the scientific community. The same could certainly be said for the case where the paradigm is a socio-political ideology.

Popper's view that we interpret the world according to laws invented by us suggests that his interpretation of the natural sciences is very close to that of Kuhn. Indeed, it can reasonably be said that the paradigm view of scientific endeavour has now gained wide acceptance; some critics, such as Feyerabend (1970), have objected to the implication that Kuhn's work is prescriptive for all the sciences rather than merely descriptive of the natural sciences, which could cause our views to become limited and stultified.

In modelling world problems, the situation to be investigated often seems to be such that there is often no single predetermined structure or paradigm on which it is efficacious, or, for reasons of acceptability desirable, to build. This is illustrated by the variety of approaches to systems analysis in general, and, for example, to particular issues such as malnutrition as discussed earlier.

The lack of any agreed 'modelling paradigm' manifests itself in the lack of agreed standards for modelling and for the assessment of models. Mar and Newell (1973) comment on a questionnaire survey, undertaken by Shubik and Brewer, of 132 modelling activities:

The results of the questionnaire indicated that, during the ten year period between assessments, the problems of poor documentation, low flow of information between model builders, and tendency for model builders to advocate selection of specific models rather than to employ a scientific basis, had not improved and probably worsened. In addition, the assessment indicated that models do not receive professional review nor are scientific standards of evaluation applied when models are examined. Furthermore, large models have found little utility since shifts in personnel, poor documentation and communication, inadequate professional review, and poor conceptualization are exaggerated with larger models. Finally, the lack of cost information to construct, operate, improve and evaluate models is poor to non-existent, thus no criteria exist to measure the effectiveness of proposed efforts.

It is generally recognized that, in all branches of science, theory advances through the social process of scientists exposing their ideas, hypotheses and experimental results to the critical examination of their colleagues. In many branches of science, this involves the extremely important social mechanism of verification by repetition of experiments and setting up experiments designed to refute hypotheses. In all branches of science, it involves the critical scrutiny of published work and of new research results. This process results in the development of a 'peer group' in each discipline and sub-discipline, competent to assess and criticize new work.

A strong peer group and the associated journals and professional organizations are not, of course, sufficient in themselves. They may become wedded to a particular narrow approach or a specialized range of techniques and fail to recognize the importance of revolutionary new ideas. In the case of social problems they may be associated with particular interests or ideologies. At times of 'paradigm change', a peer group may well be a conservative element and the impulse to new developments in theory may come from outside the discipline or peer group as previously defined. Nevertheless, even during times of change in paradigms, the behaviour of the peer group is an important element in the situation, although it may be re-instituted or revitalized.

Our conclusion from the above, then, is that some form of 'modelling paradigm', or set of paradigms, are necessary for the advance of the subject and that these can only be achieved if a mechanism by which new work can be evaluated and criticized is set up. We now move on to consider the situation in certain specific academic disciplines, with particular reference to the use made of mathematical methods. Our aim here is to present more detailed views on the controversial question of the use of quantitative techniques in the field of world problems.

PHYSICAL, BIOLOGICAL AND SOCIAL THEORIES

Many problems, particularly world problems, cross disciplinary boundaries. As we have seen, 'general systems theory' represents an attempt to formulate integrated theories of large-scale systems; but, for the moment at least, while the training of individuals is carried out almost exclusively along traditional lines, such 'interdisciplinary' studies generally proceed using teams of individuals whose expertise is in different fields. Thus, in general, world problems are only studied by using an agglomeration of concepts and methods drawn from particular disciplines. Of particular interest here is the extent to which mathematical approaches are applicable to these disciplines.

Mathematical techniques have clearly been applied most successfully in the physical sciences. The characteristics of physical systems which encourage this application are as follows:

(1) 'Physical' entities are, in general, easily identified, measured and classified and can thus be given a precise mathematical representation.
(2) Often, the system comprises few elements, or it contains a large number of interacting elements behaving in a random manner so that statistical laws permit the system to be represented by a small number of entities. Factors which cannot easily be accounted for are, of course, always present; however, it is frequently the case in physical systems that 'perturbations' are small and can be ignored, at least in the first approximation.
(3) Controlled experimentation is frequently possible. This permits isolation of the system from the effects of large perturbations and enables models and theories to be tested.
(4) The behaviour is mechanistic, i.e. there are no conscious elements present.
(5) Behaviour appears to be invariant with respect to both time and space;

thus a model constructed for a given situation at a particular time will be equally valid when the situation is reconsidered at any other place or time, whereas, in other types of system, an 'evolution' occurs during the time span of interest and real-system behaviour may change qualitatively.

The standard examples of Kuhnian 'revolutions' in physics are those which gave rise to Newtonian theory and quantum mechanics. Pre-Newtonian theory of classical motions is an excellent example of a mathematical and deterministic, yet not causal, description. Causality was introduced by Newton primarily by his use of the concept 'force'. Gravitational effects were, for example, 'due to the earth'; the effect of a force was an acceleration (Born, 1964).

In what sense did Newtonian theory correspond to reality? We quote Bellman (1971):

With success heaped upon success came extensive analysis. The formalism of Newtonian mechanics worked astonishingly well. In what sense did it represent scientific truth? Many thought it represented the ultimate theory, but there were always doubters.

Perhaps most questioned was the nature of the fundamental mechanism, gravity. What is the nature of this mysterious force that attracts two objects to each other? We really don't know. Action at a distance is as baffling to us as it was to Newton and his contemporaries.

What is important, however, to emphasize, is that the scientific world accepts this phenomenon as real despite a lack of understanding of its basic nature. The mechanism of gravity, whatever it may be, is used to construct both scientific theories and engineering systems. Observe then that lack of understanding does not materially interfere with operational utilization. This does not mean, of course, that improved understanding would not aid utilization in a number of ways, nor that we cease any efforts at understanding.

Bellman refers to '*the* ultimate theory', illustrating the point that not only was Newton's theory considered by many to represent the ultimate limit of our understanding of certain processes, but was also widely assumed to have universal validity. Such a view was held by Laplace, who considered that the entire universe consisted of bodies whose motions obeyed Newton's laws and that, in principle, if the positions and velocities of all bodies were given at a particular instant in time, the future behaviour of everything in the universe could be determined.

The emphasis of physics in the Newtonian period (up to the beginning of the twentieth century) was on causal rather than probabilistic explanation. Laws of probability were useful in many contexts, but were generally regarded as statistical approximations to the effects of causal laws. At the beginning of this century, however, a Kuhnian 'revolution' occurred: as a result of numerous contradictions between the predictions of Newtonian mechanics and the results of experiments in the atomic domain, a new theory was proposed which accounted far more successfully for these results, while Newtonian theory was retained as a limiting case applicable to the macroscopic domain. This new theory, quantum mechanics, raises the status of the laws of probability; the behaviour of sub-microscopic particles is believed to be basically statistical in character and, at the large scale, the deterministic laws of classical mechanics emerge as statistical approximations. This is precisely the converse of the situation in Newtonian theory. 'Determinism' has been abandoned and the concept of 'causality' modified so that it is understood to refer to probabilistic statements only. The initial state of a system can never be experimentally determined precisely; measurement of any parameter disturbs the system in an *unpredictable** way, resulting in uncertainty in measurement and, owing to the 'wave–particle' nature of matter, attempts to minimize this disturbance merely increase the uncertainty in the determination of a 'conjugate' parameter. Because of this uncertainty principle, *regarded as a law of nature*, the evolution of the system cannot be predicted exactly.

This interpretation is considered to be unsatisfactory by a number of physicists. While accepting that measurements inevitably affect the system, they point out that the parameters used to describe a quantum system are taken directly from classical physics and suggest the possible existence of 'hidden variables' operating deterministically in a sub-quantum domain. These give rise to the statistical laws of the higher quantum level, just as a large number of Newtonian particles behave according to statistical laws, although each particle individually is assumed to behave deterministically. This view constitutes a rejection of the 'positivist' doctrine that only observable entities should be considered. But, as Bohm (1957) points out, theoretical considerations have often led to the development of new techniques of observation.

Indeed, quantum mechanics itself developed a highly theoretical manner and a 'physical interpretation' of a key mathematical quantity was only agreed after a meeting of the leading physicists of the time (the Born interpretation of the wave function). To quote Bellman (1971):

A fascinating phenomenon, hinted at in the 19th century and explored extensively in the 20th century, particularly in the field of physics [has occurred]. This is the uncanny ability of mathematics to produce new ideas from old solely by symbol manipulation. In the field of physics this symbol manipulation has repeatedly led to the discovery of new particles and new concepts. The process is still going on, and it is possible in certain domains far outside of ordinary experience and intuition . . . Thus the pressures of reality breed fantasy which astonishingly turns out to be a new reality.

In physics, then, quantitative methods have been successful and mathematics has acquired a special status as a means of representing reality. Theoretical physicists can explain with great precision the spectra of simple atoms and molecules, engineers can simulate accurately the behaviour of some mechanical structures. But the physical systems which can be modelled so precisely are simple in comparison with almost any social process or even in comparison with many practical everyday physical phenomena. Further, very many engineering structures are designed according to the theory used to build the simulation model so in a sense both model and structure are simulations of the same theoretical assumptions. For dynamic models, it is the

*It is unpredictable because any attempt to assess the disturbance caused by the measuring apparatus involves measurements on that apparatus, which are also uncertain.

ability to identify and measure 'flows' unambiguously which is important to a successful model. Electronic circuit theory provides an ideal example. Unfortunately there are few systems that are so precisely defined.

There are of course many areas of physics where all the criteria for successful model application given earlier do not apply. In meteorology, for example, although the underlying micro-theories have been established under laboratory conditions, opportunities for experimentation on a large scale are highly constrained so that any system to be explained is likely to be very complex. (We shall consider separately the current level of theory in this subject area later.) In astrophysics and astronomy in particular, opportunities for data collection are even more constrained and, usually, a far more opportunist approach to data collections must be adopted. However, once a phenomenon has been observed, other previously unnoticed manifestations are often revealed.

In biology, the situation is rather more complex than is typically the case for physical systems. Biological systems are very diverse in character. A 'biological spectrum' can be constructed as follows: protoplasm, cells, tissues, organs, organ systems, organisms, populations, communities, ecosystems, and the biosphere (Odum, 1972). As may be expected, mathematical techniques have been most successful in describing behaviour at the 'micro' end of this spectrum, where ideas from physics or chemistry are often directly applicable. As we move towards the right-hand side of the spectrum, we find that the behaviour of the entities of interest depends in an essential way on a large number of factors. Also, there are often more measurability problems of a conceptual kind in the largest ('ecological') systems. Further, it is not obvious what is the most appropriate common unit to use to describe flows between components of an ecosytem, in analogy with the use of currency in economics: Odum (1972) stresses the value of using energy for the purpose, but this has the disadvantage that measurement is not always easy. Hence, the first two characteristics which make physical systems amenable to quantitative methods, given at the beginning of this section, are lost. For the largest systems, the third factor is also ruled out. To some extent, however, 'homeostatic mechanisms' operate in these systems; these are checks and balances brought about through the manifestation of statistical regularities in the many-entity system, as discussed previously. These regulatories are not nearly so precisely defined as those in many physical systems, however.

Historically, much effort has been devoted to the description and classification of species and, at least in the more 'macro' departments of biology, relatively little effort has been made to develop general theories of behaviour. In ecology also, which Odum considers to be that part of biology concerned with the last four levels of his classification, 'schools' have developed for the study of deserts, forests, tundra, etc. which are relatively independent of one another (Margalef, 1968). No general paradigm appears to exist in this field.

An interesting attempt at generalization has been made by Margalef (1968) with his theory of 'succession', which is analogous to the theory of evolution.

According to this theory, an ecosystem increases in diversity and biomass until a 'climax' is reached, at which the system is in equilibrium with its surroundings. Quantitative measures of 'diversity' have been proposed, but the theory is largely qualitative and it is not easy to apply directly to any given system.

Thus, although quantitative techniques are used and appear to hold promise in the ecological field, applications are made on an *ad hoc* basis, without a framework of generally accepted theory.

In the social sciences, there has been much heated discussion on the role of quantitative techniques. None of the five factors at the beginning of this section apply to a large degree for social systems. In particular, social systems are qualitatively different in that they contain the conscious actions of human beings and the underlying 'laws' appearing to govern social processes may change continuously. The need to account for conscious actions may ultimately mean that mathematical techniques, at least those techniques commonly used in the physical sciences, are of far less value in the social sciences.

The possibility that purposive human action renders attempts at forecasting in the social field futile has been expressed by Jahoda (1973). She points out that deliberate human choice can turn a forecast into a self-fulfilling or self-defeating prophecy. The supposition of the impossibility of precise deterministic forecasting in the social sciences is not surprising, since, as we have seen, it is generally believed to be impossible in the physical sciences also. However, as Jahoda points out, the fundamental difference between the disciplines is that human behaviour is directed towards a goal, explicit or implicit. 'Goals' do not exist in the natural sciences; electrons do not have free will. This opens up the form of futures studies unique to the social sciences, that of 'normative forecasting'. Given the non-deterministic nature of social futures, certain desirable futures are suggested and the feasibility and means of attaining them are explored. What is 'desirable', of course, is a matter of beliefs and values; and the obvious diversity of these is reflected in the lack of a single agreed paradigm for the social sciences. Chaney (1972) points out that, in contrast to the natural sciences, social scientists have a large number of paradigms which are competing at any given tune, and he considers that the first problem for sociologists is to sort out the various paradigms.

Not only do many conflicting value systems coexist at any one time, but the prevailing system within a given society undergoes change. This compounds the difficulties already apparent in any attempt to find fundamental parameters with which to describe society, which have been described by Rapoport (1959):

Now physics is a science in which from the very beginning a few fundamental measurable quantities were singled out for study ... when mathematical physics was extended to other classes of events ... it became necessary to isolate other variables. But the list of these physical quantities is still small ... Now the social scientist has no such list. In fairness to the social scientist, it must be admitted that he does try to invent one. The trouble is that whereas a Newton could begin with intuitively evident quantities (length as measured by sticks ...), the social scientist cannot make such a beginning. The stuff from which human relations and social structure are made is not evident intuitively. It must somehow be distilled, or abstracted, from innumerable 'events' and the selection of these events depends to a great extent on one's experiences, cultural background, and biases.

'Classification' is fundamental to the evolution of generalizable and unifying principles. However, as mentioned above, even if the social scientist is successful in obtaining a satisfactory list, he may find that, as society changes, it needs revision. Factors which are appropriate for a feudal system, for example, may be meaningless under capitalism. This can have important consequences for future studies with a distinct time horizon.

Rapoport (1959) further notes that, for a social scientist, a 'theory' is often, in effect, a set of definitions, i.e. a categorization or 'list of variables' like that referred to above. He may then seek relationships or regularities between his parameters:

However, the most serious objection to this sort of search for regularities is this ... even if the definitions satisfy every one, even if regularities reveal themselves abundantly, a catalogue of resulting equations is no more a mathematical science than a collection of bricks is a house. A mathematical science must hang together. There must be few underlying assumptions and many conclusions. The more unrelated these conclusions seem at first sight, the more powerful is the science that is able to derive them from first principles.

Difficult as the construction of such a science is in the absence of a toe hold (such as was provided for the physical scientist by the regularities in the motions of heavenly bodies), attempts in that direction have been made. The method of constructing a mathematicized social science is embodied in the concept of a so-called mathematical model.

If modelling is the main area of quantitative work, however, of what value can it be to the social sciences? Popper (1963) considers that 'the main task of the theoretical social sciences is to trace the unintended repercussions of intended human actions'. According to Forrester (1971b), computer models are ideally suited for this task; his position is that policies designed to solve problems, whether at the level of an individual company or at the national political level, often conflict with one another. By considering the policies and their interactions together in a computer model, the system can often be adequately described and solutions obtained.

Among the staunchest supporters of the extension of physics-type techniques to the social sciences are the MIT system dynamics group. Hamilton and coworkers (1969), for example, state that:

It is maintained that the role of mathematical models in the social sciences is almost the same as the role of mathematical models in the natural sciences ... As in the physical sciences, it is assumed that, if our models are useful in explaining variation in our given data, we shall be better able to predict data as yet unobserved and to institute changes that will affect as yet unobserved phenomena ... in a predictable manner. Of course, the inference from past given data to as yet unobserved data may not turn out to be correct. However, this eventuality is not peculiar to inferences about social phenomena because the possibility for error in making inferences about as yet unobserved data is present in all of science.

Some, of course, have great doubts about whether quantitative techniques are of any value in the social sciences. A leading proponent of this view is Ida Hoos (1969):

Review of completed systems analyses indicates that, far from submitting gracefully to quantitative treatment, social systems are by their very nature so laden with intangible, human variables that concentration on their measurable aspects distorts the problem and confuses the issues. One might venture the proposition that instead of assuming that social systems should be approached as though readily subject to technical treatment, those which appear technical might more appropriately be treated as social in their essence.

Others, such as Bellman (1971) and Ackoff (1960) consider that mathematics is potentially of great value to the social sciences, although new techniques may have to be developed, those taken directly from the physical sciences being inapplicable in general.

One should not forget that there are very many currently unresolved areas of physics which may well turn out to be incredibly simple (possibly within a new paradigm) but whose best represenation currently escapes our considerations. The beauty and simplicity of Kepler's laws, for example, makes a mockery of early attempts to represent the physical processes they describe. In a real sense, self-consistent theories, such as utility theory in behavioural micro-economics, attempt to portray social events with similar elegance. As in physics, however, often only limiting cases can be 'explained' and, in addition, there is far less opportunity to interpolate between the limits on the basis of empirical observation and experimentation.

What about the 'hybrid' or multidisciplinary nature of many world problems? Forrester (1971b) gives two main arguments to support his thesis that computer models are in general more satisfactory than 'mental' models:

(1) A mental model is fuzzy and incomplete. In a group discussion, different mental models are used by the participants, but assumptions and goals are rarely clearly stated. In contrast, concepts and ideas incorporated into a computer model are clearly exposed for discussion and debate.
(2) The human mind is not adapted to sensing correctly the consequences of a mental model. Unlike the computer, it is unable to trace through the sequences of implications of a given set of assumptions accurately.

Thus, according to Forrester, the computer model has the advantages of clarity and easier handling of complexity. Interestingly, computer modelling is frequently attacked on precisely these grounds. It is often claimed that mathematical models are 'clear' only to those who understand mathematics; and on the question of complexity, as early as 1957 Arrow remarked that:

The usual reaction of the 'literary' social scientist when confronted with a mathematical system designed as a model of reality is to assert that it is 'oversimplified', that it 'does not represent all the complexities of reality'. In effect, he is saying that the symbolic language in which the model is expressed is too poor to convey all the nuances of meaning which he can carry in his mind, What happens is that the very ambiguity and confusion of ordinary speech give rise to richness of meaning which surpasses, for the social scientist, the limited resources of mathematics, in which each symbol has only one meaning.*

Bellman (1971) appears to take this view:

For most ideas, mathematics is far too simple a language. We require the medium of ordinary language with its richer content, and therefore greater inherent capacity for ambiguity. That ambiguity is required for meaning, that precision requires imprecision, are paradoxes . . . the human mind, remarkably and fortunately, can cope with ambiguity.

Later, however, Bellman states that mathematics is the 'heir apparent' to the social sciences; he considers that, for many problems, the application of 'traditional' mathematical concepts and methods is based on a false view of science as representing 'absolute truth' and that new mathematical concepts are required to describe situations which are 'basically qualitative'.

Lee (1973) considers that a computer model can act as a substitute for thinking:

There is a popular illusion that confronting a computer with one's ideas enforces rigor and discipline, thereby encouraging the researcher to reject or clarify fuzzy ideas. In the very narrow sense that the human must behave exactly like a machine in order to communicate with it, this is true. But in a more useful sense, the effect is the opposite: it is all too easy to become immersed in the trivial details of working with a problem on the computer rather than think it through rationally. The effort of making the computer understand is then mistaken for intellectual activity and creative problem solving.**

Our own view is that general statements on the value of computer models are rarely useful, since the subject area and proposed utility of models are vital factors affecting their potential efficacy. We do not accept Forrester's view, which appears to suggest that computer models are always more valuable than mental models, nor the attitude described by Arrow, which implies that, since models are simplifications, they are necessarily useless. We believe that models often can be of value, provided that the dangers of excessive modelling zeal, such as those pointed out by Bellman and Lee, are recognized. On the question of explicitness, it is often true that a full presentation of a model enables a group, unconnected with those who constructed it, to analyse the work in a less ambiguous way than is possible with a verbal treatment. The risks of misunderstanding and misinterpretation are largely overcome. However, in two other ways, full clarity has not been achieved. First, there is the problem to which we have already referred, namely that of comprehension by those not familiar with mathematical notation, who would scarcely be persuaded that

*Reprinted from 'Mathematical Models in the Social Sciences', by J. Kemeny and J. L. Snell by permission of the MIT Press, Cambridge, Mass.
**Reprinted by permission of the Journal of the American Institute of Planners, vol. 39, no. 3, May 1973.

models afford a clearer presentation of ideas and may complain that an attempt is being made to 'blind them with science'. This problem is particularly acute in those cases where models are expected to be of use in public policy, both because the policy maker is unlikely to put trust in a model he does not understand and because public debate is likely to be restricted. This problem is more fully explored in Chapter 6. Secondly, it is doubtful whether many mathematicians, used to studying equations written in closed form, would regard a large-scale computer model as 'clear'. Indeed, it seems that to check out even some of the implications of a large-scale model requires a great deal of work and even then one is left with the feeling that full understanding has not been, and cannot be, achieved. It may not be enough to understand the individual relationships comprising the model in isolation; the connections between these relationships are profoundly important to model behaviour and it is extremely difficult to grasp totally their effects. Whether these 'disadvantages' outweigh the 'advantages' depends on the type of model and the use to which it is to be put. Loss of ambiguity may be of first importance in testing consistency of theories; lack of public comprehension may be fatal for policy making.

As we have seen, one important advantage that large-scale models are argued to have over mental models, according to Forrester (1971b), is that they can show that social systems behave in a 'counter-intuitive' way and can indicate that the most appropriate remedies to problems are often not those which seem intuitively obvious to decision makers. This assertion is based on the fact that a large model treats the interactions between a number of variables simultaneously; it is claimed that only such an 'overall' view can reveal the true consequences of policies which are often implemented from a much narrower perspective, without a full awareness by the decision maker of possible ramifications in parts of the system with which he may not be familiar. If a given policy directly improves a particular situation A, it is often implemented, despite the fact that it also causes changes in a part B of the system, which in turn cause a worsening of A, which may be more significant than the direct improvement. As a particular example, Forrester states in his *Urban Dynamics* (1969) that a policy frequently adopted to ameliorate urban decay is the provision of low-cost housing, whereas Forrester's model indicates that this merely causes a migration into the city of more people, which exacerbates the unemployment problem and eventually worsens the urban problem as a whole. Precisely the same kind of argument was used in respect of the MIT world models.

The argument is really nothing more than an emphasis on the need to take a 'holistic' view, particularly in the field of policy. It asserts simply that, by so doing, one obtains different results from those obtained by a more restricted viewpoint and that the former are more likely to be valid. As with the 'clarity' argument, it seems to us that generalization is difficult. In theory, the argument is convincing; in practice, bearing in mind that a 'holistic' representation demands complexity and the use of theoretical ideas of varying quality, it is quite possible that 'noise' may be introduced and that the results may be entirely spurious. Forrester's highly controversial conclusions on urban problems depend on the quality of the data he used and on the fact that his holistic theory was in fact restricted. Further, it should be pointed out that, given the important assumptions incorporated into a large-scale model, its behaviour is often quite predictable and is not 'counter-intuitive' at all. The pessimistic estimates of natural resource reserves in the MIT world models, for example, imply immediately that industrial production must eventually decline. We would maintain that Forrester's advocacy of the 'systems view-point' is justified, but that he seriously underrates the problems involved in its application.

ORGANIZATIONAL ISSUES IN WORLD MODEL BUILDING

Large-scale models, such as global models, are particularly demanding in that decisions about their construction involve a large number of factors and that these are inseparable from themselves and from issues such as model applica-tion we discuss in other chapters. This conclusion has several implications for the organization and structure of the institutions needed to support global modelling projects.

As was suggested at the beginning of this chapter, one of the major features of world modelling studies is their 'hybrid' nature, i.e. they require professional expertise from a number of different academic disciplines. This entails a high level of cooperation between researchers. A second issue of organization is the relationship of the modelling team and its research results to the relevant 'peer groups'. For interdisciplinary research, the peer group activity is rather poor, which is in part due to the large quantity of documentation associated with the publication of a serious world model. A third issue is that of the relationship of the model (and researchers within the peer group) to society as a whole via policy-making bodies and, directly or indirectly, through propa-ganda activities. We leave this last issue until Chapter 6 and here consider questions of modelling group organization and the publication of research findings.

Interdisciplinary research is never easy, even when the disciplines involved are few and relatively closely related. In attempting to build a model of the world nominally purporting to include all its important interactions, the various disciplines involved bring obvious problems of communication. In addition to this, world model building is a highly 'political' activity in that it is concerned with rather fundamental human values, to which ideas of 'right' or 'wrong' in an absolute or even in the 'scientific' sense of peer group consensus cannot be satisfactorily ascribed.

Good interdisciplinary communication within a team usually requires a fairly long-standing working relationship, often between individuals and members of the associated disciplines. Interdisciplinary research usually consists of individuals having a sufficient grasp of a number of fields to be able to coordinate ideas and make constructive associations. The construction of a world model is a time-consuming activity and most of the modelling groups discussed in Chapter 2 have 10 to 20 members. For a single researcher to build a serious model would probably require more than a 'new Renaissance man'. The threshold level of competence of individual team members is both the ability to understand the arguments on each issue and an awareness in each field, combined with the ability to communicate clearly their own field of interest. Even if every researcher is not involved directly in the construction of the model, they should all be able to follow arguments concerned with its organization and at least be able to reassure themselves that the equations of the model and its computed results do, in fact, correspond to their proposals! In essence, this means being able to ask the right questions and understand the answers.

Some authors (for example, Benyon (1972)) argue that models are a good communicative medium within an interdisciplinary team. Some evidence, such as that of Chartier (1972) and Lewis and Wentworth (1971) noted in Appendix A, indicates that this point requires further empirical justification. More convincing are the arguments that model building helps to structure debate so that the process of modelling, rather than the model itself, may contribute the major benefit.

The threshold size of a team must be such that all aspects of the issue on which attention is focused are covered. Often, for personal reasons or reasons of project organization, the research team is subdivided into smaller groups (often 2 or 3 workers) and maintaining continuity across the whole project can present difficulties. In the case of the Mesarovic–Pestel model, for example, construction of the model is divided between the United States and Europe. To maintain a high level of mutual understanding (providing structural continuity and a common technical approach), a fair degree of interchangeability between subgroups is needed.

Benyon (1972) considers that there is a definite procedure that a large interdisciplinary team should follow, and that both the model and the team should be organized in a hierarchy. While we consider this to be valid in some instances, it seems more likely that the organization of each team should be considered on its own merits; in many ways our own experience suggests the reverse of Benyon's proposition.

A most important ingredient for successful cooperation in a world modelling effort seems to be a compatible political and value framework among the researchers. Many of the problems which have arisen in various modelling efforts come from this source and from questions of status within the group. Perhaps, given human nature, these kinds of problems are inevitable and, probably, the most efficient team would consist of a few highly expert, hardworking individuals of a similar political outlook. Unfortunately, if the stability of a group is enhanced, by achieving internal consensus, the likelihood of producing a model widely acceptable outside the group is reduced. This reinforces arguments regarding the need for pluralism (i.e. for several groups to be involved, mutually criticizing each other's work) in this kind of activity. Clearly if, as we suggest later, the building of a satisfactory long-range forecasting model for use in public policy is a long-term activity, then many issues of team organization are likely to arise. We consider these will only be ultimately resolved by the evolution of an effective interdisciplinary peer group.

For an academic peer group to be effective and for it to communicate well to outside audiences in government and among the lay public, satisfactory modes of publication are required. One of the major criticisms made by academics of the *The Limits to Growth* exercise was that the *Technical Report* containing the details of the computer calculations, its data and validation was not made publicly available until over one year after the highly publicized first presentation of the work. To some degree the delay was due to the vast amount of documentation inevitable for a model of world scope. The *Technical Report* consisted of over one thousand pages. *Preliminary* presentations of the Mesarovic–Pestel and Bariloche models at the International Institute for Applied Systems Analysis each lasted several days. How to publicize world models without losing their intended message, while offering satisfactory detailed justification, is quite clearly a major challenge to world modellers.

Technically, the publication of models in such a way that they can be readily assessed in detail and constructively criticized by other modellers is not easy. Because the media used for intermediate storage of data and steps in modelling are unusual (e.g. computer media such as tapes, discs, massive print-out), full publication in sufficient depth for independent reproduction of the work elsewhere does not match happily with the traditional scientific paper. Often, work is only reproducible with difficulty, not because of language representation, but because some language implementations on particular machine configurations are unique. This is clearly an area where publication standards and issues of relocatability for purposes of assessment must be explored as part of the constraints upon choice of modelling approach.

At present, there is a lack of uniformity of presentation between publishers and journals; the ideal of a comprehensive verbal description, combined with a full program listing, is rarely found. A possible compromise between the need for work to be available for evaluation and the expense of full publication is that a full verbal description of the work should be published, together with details of programming language, type of computer required, core used etc., and that readers should be given some means of obtaining the full listing, e.g. from a library run by the journal concerned.

Some researchers have continued to make amendments to their models and it is difficult to identify any 'final version' of their work. Critical analysis of, for example, the World 3 model was hampered since continual revisions of the work were produced after the publication of *The Limits to Growth* (see Cole and Curnow, 1973). To permit serious evaluation, modellers must be prepared to provide definitive statements at some stage.

It may be argued that at the current state-of-the-art, such detailed critical evaluation is not needed. For example, Cole and coworkers (1973) and others have argued that the general conclusions of Worlds 2 and 3 were evident given their underlying assumptions. The computer model served only to disguise the assumptions and provide an aura of spurious authenticity. Despite this, it appeared that the only *convincing* rebuttal was to run the model and demonstrate its inadequacies. Nevertheless, it is hoped that future models (and indeed the present models) will deserve, and receive, detailed investigation. There may be little hope in the real world of sufficient independent reproduction of the work elsewhere for early creation of an effective peer group, as has been normal in most scientific disciplines.

There are a number of other reasons apart from the technical and interdisciplinary issues we have mentioned which make the assessment of large-scale models difficult. Unlike 'big science' (another area where reproduction of results is difficult because of the high cost), much of the information which one would like to put into a model (for example, mineral deposits) is at present guarded for economic or strategic reasons. For this reason, modelling projects built in government departments, such as the UK Department of the Environment model, and most likely to receive long-term funding, may be least open to final evaluation. However, we will argue later that we believe such difficulties can be overcome.

5

Technical Issues of World Models and Modelling

In this chapter we examine the process of constructing a computer model and discuss some of the technical problems and options which must, or should, be considered by the modeller. Our aim is not to 'instruct' on how to build a world model (since we assume at least an elementary knowledge of technical matters), but to point to issues and comment on the merits of some of the methods which are used or are available at present.

To provide a framework for this discussion, it is useful to consider the process of modelling as comprising a number of interlinked activities as follows:

(1) Issues are designated as problems and numerical data believed to represent aspects of those issues, and algebraic relationships between them, are chosen.

(2) The relationships are matched to the data (i.e. calibrated).

(3) This model is translated, usually via the compiler program of a computer, into a numerical digital form and the results are generated by successive computation.

(4) These results, accompanied by varying amounts of supporting argument, constitute the findings.

This simple description of the process of building a computer model is shown diagrammatically in Figure 7.

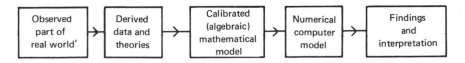

Figure 7. Model building activities

In practice, the construction of a model is never the simple step-to-step process implied by this diagram; rather, it is an iterative process, by which

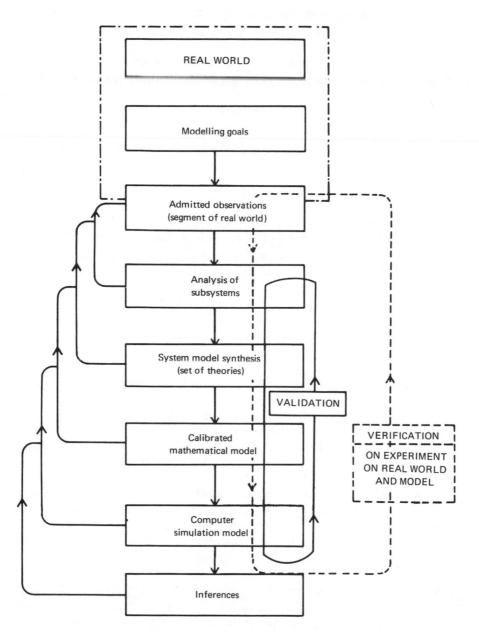

Figure 8. Model building as an iterative process

the results obtained at later stages may require modifications to be made in earlier procedures. For example, the model results may indicate that the theories on which it is based are inconsistent, indicating the necessity for a revision of an earlier part of the process. Further, the diagram does not bring out sufficiently clearly the particular stages where technical choices, with which we are here concerned, have to be made.

Remembering that, in representing any system or process, we inevitably look at it from a particular point of view (i.e. from within a specific paradigm) and, from Ackoff's definition of a model (p. 33), for the particular purpose of highlighting certain issues, we choose Figure 8 as the 'model of the modelling process' most appropriate for our purposes.

The technical issues we wish to discuss are related to the stages in the modelling process shown in the diagram as follows:

(1) The choice of modelling goals includes the choice of phenomena to be highlighted and the proposed application of the model.

(2) Admitted observations determine, and are determined by, the choice of system boundaries, made in the light of modelling goals.

(3) An analysis of subsystems requires consideration of suitable subsystem boundaries, which is closely related to the problem of determining an appropriate level of aggregation.

(4) System—model synthesis involves the selection of appropriate theories of system behaviour and the construction of plausible relationships from data.

(5) The translation of these relationships into a calibrated mathematical model involves the consideration of incorporating uncertainty into the structure.

(6) For a computer simulation model, choices of programming language, integration method etc. must be made.

(7) Inferences from the model are necessarily speculative, the issue here being that of the grounds on which they can be justified.

(8) Decisions must be taken on the extent to which model testing, i.e. the processes of validation and verification, are worthwhile and feasible.

Implicitly, all methods of forecasting involve making choices and assumptions corresponding to those listed. In mathematical modelling the method of analysis is made more explicit than with other methods; this does not necessarily mean that the theoretical assumptions underlying the model are exposed more clearly, although it does enable us to discuss individual steps in the activity more easily.

Even Figure 8 is not complete in that the impact of the model on the social process, and the feedback response of the latter on the model or on the real world system it describes, are not considered. For the moment, however, we will conduct our discussion with reference to Figure 8.

MODELLING GOALS AND ADMITTED OBSERVATIONS—THE SELECTION OF APPROPRIATE DATA

Here some observations will be made regarding the process of selecting parameters and data. Our object is to point out some features of this process and some dangers inherent in it. It should be remembered that, however a rigorous discussion of a problem is to be approached, by formal modelling methods or any other, suitable data are essential. What is peculiar to mathematical modelling exercises is that more complete and coherent data are required.

First, as earlier chapters have made clear, the selection of data and parameters to represent a system is highly subjective and will reflect just one of many possible perceptions of the issues at hand. Consider, for example, a model concerned with the prediction of economic welfare. It is likely that a choice of gross national product as an indicator of welfare would call upon different mechanisms to be represented, and might indeed project a different future, from one based on, say, the income of the lowest 5% of the population or on the disparities between income levels. This issue is clearly pertinent to world models; Forrester and Meadows chose to concentrate on 'physical' factors in their models, while later efforts have emphasized other parameters.

The problem becomes especially acute in the building of forecasting models when the possible long-term trend in issues of fairly recent or of periodic concern are to be considered. As described in Chapter 1, concern with the environment is not new and, in the past, technological or social change has reduced the harmful impact of pollutants of various kinds. Thus an important question (which was critical to the 'limits to growth' debate) is whether recent and often poorly quantified trends in data signify the beginning of a long-term trend or are merely part of bounded but oscillitory dynamic behaviour (such as trade cycles). Dator (1972) has discussed the problem of interpreting time series data, pointing out the great uncertainties that must arise when extrapolating this over long periods.

As remarked earlier, without an underlying theory to explain a trend, there is little hope of making a successful forecast. Although naive extrapolation methods (such as the Box–Jenkins' prediction technique (1970)) are atheoretical (in that no explicit theory of the process under observation is employed) and are adequate for some short-term forecasting, they may be completely misleading in the longer term and give no insight into the effect of alternative policy options.

While the modeller would appear to have considerable freedom in choosing his parameters, certain constraints do operate in practice. The most important is that many of the data and theories he may require have been gathered or derived for other purposes. Data have yet to be collected specifically for world models and it seems inevitable that any parameterization regarded as 'optimal' will have to be compromised to enable use to be made of previous work.

In the case of world models particularly, it is likely that no one data source will be adequate. Rather, several sources will almost always be required, especially when, as is often the case, different subsystems have been mapped onto different disciplinary or application areas. As a result, there is a great danger of incoherence and inconsistency among the data used in the model. Even within a particular subsystem, the available data are often of poor quality, sparse, inconsistent, and may have been distorted for political reasons. In the MIT world models, for example, the lack of time-series data forced the researchers to assume that global average development paths follow the course implied by current cross-sectional data taken from nations at various stages of development. This is a common but cavalier assumption.

In practice, then, a modeller seeking to represent a system is more restricted than he may realize, or wish to be, in choosing his parameters and data. This choice, which constitutes what we call the admitted observations, depends on his own preconceptions of what are the essential characteristics of the system, which in turn depend on the influence of previous work and accepted theories. It also depends on what sets of data are available, those sets themselves being conditioned by different, possibly contradictory, theories. It is difficult for a modeller to be 'original' in these matters; the important point is that he should recognize that his perspective is necessarily particular and restricted. The best that can be done is to define the system, through the selection of parameters, in terms of the modelling goals, and show the possible effects of other choices to minimize the risk of falsely including or excluding information in the model. By experimenting with the designation of system boundaries some demonstration can be made that an optimal choice of parameters has been achieved. Although the construction of a *world* model ought to reduce the need for this, in practice, as we have emphasized, any model is only a partial representation, so problems of inclusion remain. There are no techniques which can guarantee perfection in the process of parameter and data selection in a complex model.

SUBSYSTEMS AND AGGREGATION

World models usually consist of a set of linked subsystems comprising conventional economic, demographic or ecological sectors. The reasons for such a division are essentially pragmatic. They allow the problem to be considered in terms of smaller, more manageable units which can, in the first instance, be studied independently by individual members of the modelling team with expertise in particular fields. In practice, the choice of subsystem boundaries is correspondingly a matter of convenience, dictated by available data and proposed application, rather than a statistically determined best choice (as might emerge from a cluster or factor analysis). Some operational considerations should be borne in mind, however, when selecting appropriate divisions for a given total system. Clymer (1969) suggests the following:

(1) Time and space scales. For example, it is undesirable to attempt to represent 'micro' and 'macro' processes, or processes with very different characteristic time constants, in the same sub-model, since widely varying levels of description can cause great validation problems.
(2) Spatial location. It is usually convenient, in a regionally disaggregated model, to describe each region by its own sub-model.

(3) Functional level. Where the system under investigation has a 'hierarchical' structure, it is useful to allow each level in the hierarchy (such as each trophic level in an ecological system) its own sub-model.

(4) Accessibility for measurement. It is important that data should be available corresponding to the variables forming inputs and outputs to individual sub-models, so that these can be independently validated.

(5) Degree of coupling. Strongly coupled parts of a system are normally kept within the same sub-system, so that the division is a 'natural' one reflecting to some extent the nature of the real system.

(6) Available expertise. The division most closely corresponding to the areas of expertise of individuals working on the project should be selected, to make best use of available skills.

Generally, these recommendations are compatible; a division based on (5), for example, will, normally, automatically satisfy (2), (3) and (6); where incompatibilities arise, the issue is best settled by trial and error.

At some stage, of course, individual sub-models have to be combined and it is often found that the results are disappointing. A model built up systematically from well accredited and carefully calibrated single relationships or simple sub-models may not give a sensible total model. This has been the experience of many econometricians; some of the best known economic models have suffered in this way. What is happening here, the danger of which we have already indicated, is that information has been wrongly included or excluded from the model in one or more ways. The forecasts of the total model may, in exceptional cases, be quite misleading. This deficiency could be reduced by calibrating the model as a whole, thus subsuming omissions and structural faults. Indeed, it is usually necessary to do this to some extent. As the Mesarovic–Pestel group discovered, to produce a population model 'robust' to highly asymmetric age distributions (as found in Latin America), one-year cohorts have to be considered. Clearly this level of detail throughout a model in many of its subsystems would be unmanageable even if the data were available. In any model a compromise with regard to detail and approximation has to be reached.

This example shows that the analysis of subsystems cannot be divorced from a consideration of the appropriate level of disaggregation, e.g. the number of world regions to be considered, or the number of age cohorts within the population sub-model. Indeed, division into subsystems can be regarded as equivalent to disaggregation, or at least as one phase of it.

The final level of aggregation should, in the interests of simplicity and manageability, be as high as possible, consistent with two requirements, related respectively to the proposed utility of the model and its empirical validity. These are that the level of detail must be great enough to permit the model to perform its preassigned function, and that futher disaggregation does not markedly affect the results obtained. As an example, consider the MIT models viewed as having been constructed as aids to decision making.

The level of aggregation is so high that a non-existent 'global decision maker' is required to implement their recommendations for avoiding catastrophe and it can therefore be argued that insufficient attention has been paid to the practicalities of policy making when choosing the aggregation level. Secondly, as Cole and Curnow (1973) demonstrated, the models give markedly different results when disaggregated into two world regions, which casts considerable doubt on the reliability of the general behaviour shown by the aggregated models.

This crucial test of further disaggregation requires some care, however; if poor data is used, 'noise' can be introduced and the more highly disaggregated model can be a poorer representation of the system than the original. The test cannot, of course, be applied *a priori* and can only be used to justify a level of aggregation after the event, i.e. when the model is built and results are available. Some indications, however, may be available in advance on whether a model will be 'robust' to further disaggregation in this sense. A set of parameters can be expected to merit aggregation if they have similar properties and are independent (in which case their properties are additive) or if they are numerous and interact in a random manner (when statistical laws may be used to give rather precise estimates of aggregate behaviour, as in the statistical mechanics of gases). A detailed discussion of this is given by Sharp (1974). In the last analysis, however, *a posteriori* justification is always required.

SYSTEM–MODEL SYNTHESIS: TREATMENT OF DATA AND UNCERTAINTY

Several methods exist to aid the transformation of a set of admitted observations and theories into a coherent mathematical representation. For single-variable or simple multivariable models, there are various statistical tests which permit the 'significance' or validity of the curve fitting to be assessed. The object here is to 'explain' the maximum amount of variation of the data with the least number of parameters—which might be considered a primary goal of scientific endeavour.

Some of the most sophisticated attempts at parameter estimation have been in the field of urban spatial location and transportation modelling. Curry (1972), for example, emphasizes the problem of calibration that arises when the real-world distribution of phenomena is dominated by the effects considered in the model (thus making it hard to obtain an independent sample). Attempts at calibration of dynamic spatial models are relatively few (see, for example, Sayer (1974)). Dynamic models which are not disaggregated spatially are more common in econometric studies.

Statistical techniques are being used to some degree by most world modellers, as by the Bariloche and Mesarovic–Pestel groups, but were hardly used in the MIT models. The statistical methods mentioned above are subject to certain rather severe limitations; in particular, their use requires, in practice, that the model structure be linear, a feature that Forrester (1971b) appears to regard as fatally restrictive; in his view models should reflect the 'multiple-feedback-loop and nonlinear nature of real systems'. Thus system dynamicists such as Forrester sacrifice the possibility of using statistical techniques to validate their results for the flexibility afforded by the nonlinear 'look-up tables' of the 'system dynamics' method.

The attraction of nonlinear representations, in general, is that they may capture the apparent nonlinearities inherent in social systems. The virtue of linear models is that model behaviour is easier to comprehend, interpret and test. The real trade-off being made in deciding on a linear or nonlinear form is between modelling 'simplicity' in terms of reducing parameters to a minimum and 'realism' by simulating as closely as possible the observed behaviour.

A means of determining whether significant gains are made by using a nonlinear representation is to linearize the model after construction. This process has been performed by Rademaker (1974) and others on the MIT models, and it appears that nonlinearity introduced an unnecessary complication into many of the relationships.

Over any given portion of a model's regime of validity, it will be approximately linear, so that full linearization and the use of techniques developed for linear models are a useful but limited way of gaining understanding of nonlinear model behaviour (Kruskal (1965)). The 'look-up tables' used in system dynamics models do in fact represent a 'partial linearization' in that the relationships are represented by a sequence of linear sections. It has been shown by van der Corinten and de Jong (cited by Rademaker, 1972) that replacing these junctions by smooth nonlinear relationships can give markedly different results. It therefore appears that in some circumstances such models behave more like linear than nonlinear models.

Young (1973), while accepting that nonlinear relationships are useful in describing physical systems, does not feel that their use is justified in poorly understood social systems. In particular, he maintains that a 'law of large systems' frequently operates in which the overall response characteristics of complex systems are often quite simple and can adequately be generated by a linear model.

Nonlinearity does appear to be fundamental to many physical and ecological processes (when, for example, it represents the impact of short-range effects on long-range phenomena). Hence, although there are sound reasons to justify the use of linear models at the outset, experimentation with nonlinear forms will often be required.

Whatever form is chosen, the structure and parameters used can never be known precisely. Thus the incorporation of uncertainty into the calibrated mathematical model must be considered.

Uncertainty in results may arise from two main sources: uncertainty of measurement and inherent stochastic fluctuations. Uncertainty of measurement, i.e. the margin of error in data used to calibrate relationships, can be quite considerable in world models. To take an example, the UK census of population, perhaps the most accurate in the world, is acknowledged to have up to 0.75% error on the total recorded figure (subtotals may have a much higher fractional error). In developing countries, sampling errors may be considerably higher. Notwithstanding these errors, it is probably true that population data are among the most accurate available to world modellers.

In view of this situation, data uncertainty should be recognized at all stages in the modelling process. As suggested earlier, disaggregation beyond a certain level may be positively detrimental unless data is of the required quality. Within an agreed model structure, measurement errors may be presented by distributing each of the specific values given in a model's initial conditions by a random distribution covering the range of uncertainty; successive model runs then translate these distributions into output uncertainty (Mar and Newell, 1973). The pragmatic way of looking at uncertainty is to explore the *consequences* of possible errors in the data used, the possibilities for which are discussed when we consider model testing.

Many features of the real world appear to be subject to stochastic fluctuations. Climate is an example; while our description of its fluctuations as 'stochastic' arises from our present inability to make accurate forecasts rather than from an inherent feature of the real system, our current lack of knowledge demands that they be treated as such. Stochastic effects may be approximated by several techniques, e.g. by making repeated runs of a model, sampling from random distributions to approximate errors, noise or uncertainty, and establishing average values produced over all runs. Few of the models we have examined, of the world model type, or even within a specialist discipline or application, have paid much attention to this aspect of modelling.

Modellers may be remiss here, for as Young (1973) has pointed out, many apparently robust models are suspect when the consequences of uncertainty are examined. While the lack of consideration of this question may be caused by an exceedingly slow diffusion of techniques from statistical methodology into modelling, or by the fact that these techniques may be expensive and time-consuming, it may also reflect a conscious or subconscious realization that many models do not give unique inferences if uncertainty is allowed.

Where modellers do not account for the effects of statistical variation in parameters, the implicit assumption is being made that simply taking the average or 'most likely' value of all the parameters will give the same average value for the model solution as would be obtained if random or stochastic effects are included. This is usually not so, since contributions arising from error terms in the algebraic expansion of a relationship do not necessarily cancel one another, as would be required for the assumption to hold.

Many models, including the MIT world models, are based on ordinary (or partial) differential or difference equations, which are deterministic in character. These techniques have, of course, been extremely fruitful in the natural sciences, where the system of interest can frequently be isolated from stochastic influences to a high degree. Forrester's world model, for example, can be viewed as 'clockwork' in its operation. Stochastic and probablistic influences of the real world can be incorporated into a difference-equation representation. Most simulation languages, including DYNAMO (the language of the system dynamics methodology developed at MIT, and used in the Forrester–Meadows work), offer facilities for achieving this, although they are not used in either model.

Another method of avoiding the spurious precision associated with much of the work performed in modelling world problems is by the use of 'gaming'. This approach has been used extensively, in particular in the hierarchical Mesarovic–Pestel world model. Here an operator (or operators) observes the time evolution of the model and inserts 'policy decisions' which influence its development. The main motive for this, as discussed in Chapter 2, is to separate the 'mechanical' features of the system which are incorporated in a deterministic model from those often intangible factors depending to a great extent on human action. A fuller discussion of the gaming approach is given in Appendix A.

An approach related to gaming is that of 'goal seeking', as adopted by the Bariloche and Japanese groups; recognizing that humanity can choose between alternative futures, an 'objective' or 'goal' function is chosen whose optimum value represents the desired future; this function is then optimized, subject to recognized constraints, and the feasibility of the desired future can be estimated. As Jeffers (1973) has pointed out, it can also be used to indicate which constraint is the most important in inhibiting the achievement of a desired future. Such a technique is equivalent to a gaming method, with the difference that precise specification of the goal of the player (or players) is required in advance.

This technique is, of course, borrowed from control engineering and, indeed, many world modellers were initially system scientists of control. Control concepts are often useful for clarifying thinking about objectives, especially if the control subsystem is built in terms of parameters normally recognized as policy variables, i.e. they are manipulable in the real world. In practice, the method seems more appropriate to systems with a complexity far below that of global models, such as air traffic control or river authority structures, where the 'physical' system described is relatively well defined and unambiguous and the 'decisions' to be taken are reasonably straightforward.

The discussion of choice of technique has not yet touched upon the choice of tool, such as type of computer or programming language. In theory, and to a large extent in practice, the two are independent; the above choices of technique can, in general, be deployed on many types of computer and in any of several available languages. The use of a computer inevitably introduces further error into a model and machine capacity can sometimes be a limiting factor, but problems introduced at this stage in the modelling process are usually relatively minor. For this reason, and because the discussion is rather technical, we have covered this topic in Appendix B.

MODEL TESTING

It is convenient to divide the methods available for testing a model into two groups. The first is designed to show that the model provides a consistent and rigorous representation of the 'admitted data' on which it is based. We use the word *validation* to describe this process of demonstrating internal consistency. This process is not sufficient, since a model must also provide a satisfactory representation outside this range of validity in order to be useful as a forecasting device. We use the term *verification* to describe the process of demonstrating that a model can show behaviour similar to that which is occurring, or can occur, in the real world, beyond that already reflected in the admitted data. This is fundamental to the utility of modelling in the sense that, unless model behaviour can be shown to be generalizable to some degree, no contribution to finding a solution to the problems with which it is concerned has been achieved.

For the purpose of clarification, therefore, we shall distinguish between the concepts of validation and verification. It should be noted that current USA practice, which is gaining ground, is to consider both under the one label of validation. However, for world models, the distinction is important and we retain here the original UK practice based on the Oxford English Dictionary definitions: 'validation'—being well grounded in principles or evidence; 'verification'—proven to be true by evidence. In the physical sciences verification has formed the heart of scientific method by taking the form of a critical prediction from theory to be followed by the corresponding critical experiment in the real world.

In practice, model testing cannot be entirely separated from model construction and we have already discussed some techniques which would be included under the term 'validation'. Such techniques include the following:

(1) 'Robustness' to level of aggregation. Checking that further disaggregation does not markedly influence any conclusions which may be drawn from the model provides a test of model structure. The problems involved in this process should be remembered, however; it is necessary that the disaggregated data should be drawn from the same set as that used to calibrate the original model, so that it is consistent with it and is not subject to a higher level of uncertainty.
(2) *Sensitivity analysis*. If the conclusions drawn from a model are to be in any sense valid, they must be independent of variations in model output resulting from different values that can be chosen for the input data, within their confidence limits. Ideally, the model should be run with all combinations of such values, but in practice many model structures demand compromise on this issue.

Sensitivity analysis, by showing the extent of variations in output from possible data deficiencies, can indicate those parts of the model where good data is of particular importance; also, if it is found that output is insensitive to particular parameters, it suggests that these variables may be superfluous. In a nonlinear model, however, care should be taken in discarding parameters found to be insensitive over one particular model range, or in assuming that extreme inaccuracy due to errors in a particular parameter makes the results meaningless for all periods.

Both Forrester and Meadows, in their world models, employ one-parameter-at-a-time sensitivity testing, which is in general quite inappropriate to a highly interacting model involving considerable nonlinearities. Scolnik (1973) has shown how, with less than 5% variation in any of the initialization parameters (and with an average change of only 0.75%), World 3 gave totally different patterns of 'results'. As the SPRU critique (Cole and coworkers, 1973) argued, such uncertainty in these parameters is not at all impossible. The technique used by Scolnik was essentially that of linearization of the initial trajectory of the model obtained by maximizing the population prediction at the year 2300. The so-called collapse of population of the World 3 model was delayed until well beyond the year 2300 and was then extremely gentle in form. Systematic sensitivity analysis, however, is an extremely difficult and lengthy procedure on nonlinear models, and often it is necessary to linearize a model in order to study its behaviour under different assumptions.

(3) *2-sample test*. This involves splitting the available data into two equal parts, using one part for model-building and the other as a comparison against model output. This appears at first sight wasteful of scarce and costly data, but it is a powerful test. The method can be applied in two ways. First, the original data can be split at random into two halves, using one for calibration and the other for validation; this is a crude way of avoiding the necessity of rigorously checking the consequences of data uncertainty. The second approach is to split the available time-series data into two successive time halves, the earlier part being used for calibration and the later for validation. This version of the technique assumes that the same mechanisms were dominant during the two time periods represented by the sets of data, which is the assumption made when the model is projected into the future.

It often turns out that the more recent half of the available data is of better quality and it may be more sensible to use it for calibration. If the model is deterministic, it can then be 'run backwards' by reversing the sign of the time increment and its ability to regenerate the earlier data tested. This 'backcasting' technique was used on the MIT models by the Sussex team (Cole and co-workers, 1973). The method has given rise to some controversy (Meadows and coworkers, 1973), and in view of the continuing interest (see, for example, *The Ecologist*, July 1974) in the debate, a brief discussion is in order here.

The real world does not run backwards for very good thermodynamic reasons; and neither can models of social and other processes that contain an explicit representation of homeostatis. Models like the MIT models do *not* represent self-regulating processes and ought to run backwards if the calculations are performed precisely. The MIT models consist of a set of values for state variables from which quantities are added or subtracted at each iteration. If the models do not run backwards it is not for any fundamental theoretical reason but because the particular numerical integration routine used is not completely accurate. In the DYNAMO programming method the simplest possible Euler routine is used (see Cole and Curnow, 1973). While the backcasting test is not general, since there may often be a large number of numerical instabilities arising from approximations in the computation present in a multiple-loop feedback model which cannot be controlled, it can be a useful test for examining long-term models. There are few possibilities for validating a long-term model of a unique system and backcasting provides a relatively straightforward test. Analytical justification for the technique has been presented elsewhere in some detail (Cole and Curnow, 1973; Sharp, 1974). Analysis by an MIT author (Wright, 1973) confirmed the Sussex finding and provides a rebuttal of Meadow's claim that the backcasting anomaly is 'spurious' and arises because of a mis-specification in Forrester's model.

(4) *Integration methods*. Errors arising from the use of approximate methods of integration in the computerized model should be small compared with errors caused by data and structure. Many integration techniques (besides the most commonly used Euler and Runge–Kutta routines), of different accuracy, are available, and if there is doubt as to the computing accuracy at least two methods should be used. If the difference in output is small, this provides some demonstration that integration errors are unimportant.

Verification, as we have said, involves seeking fresh evidence to support the model and is a stronger test of a model. If the model has surplus content (which is an essential prerequisite for a forecasting model), the behaviour pattern may be in some way unexpected. This usually leads to a conscious search for a demonstration of that unexpected behaviour, either in some manifestation not previously taken into account, or in a period of deliberate experimentation or observation.

Controlled experimentation is, of course, relatively difficult and usually impossible for many aspects of social systems (although small-scale social experiments are a common feature of societies), and for large-scale ecological or physical systems, all of which are relevant to world models. Since large-scale experimentation is not practicable, it would seem that there is no choice but to await *a posteriori* justification for simulation models, which may be of little practical use for a model designed to forecast 30 years ahead. However, since the purpose of many models is to provide a basis upon which methods of control can be tested, and then applied to the real world, the monitoring of the success of those control procedures provides some evidence as to the value of the model for this purpose, as much as to its closeness to 'reality' in a theoretical sense.

An additional problem, which is particularly acute in the verification of very simplified models, such as highly aggregated models of world problems, is that such models are clearly approximations and the process of verification (or falsification) is correspondingly approximate. Immediately this raises the issue of false acceptance of a bad model and false rejection of a good model. Perhaps the most useful concept to be deployed in this context is to search consciously for other models which would give equally acceptable fits as the model being considered. This purely technical issue reinforces the case for pluralism in model building which has been advocated elsewhere in this book.

Even though verification is a necessary step, it is not, in one sense, sufficient. Total sufficiency can only be tested through all possible experience and our knowledge of systems suggests that the adequacy of a model or theory changes, or may change, in time. It is tempting to ascribe this phenomenon entirely to the changing purposive actions of human beings in a social process, but this in turn is essentially a non-verifiable hypothesis, adequate though it may prove for purposes of hindsight discussion. Even theories in physical science can never be totally verified and confidence in them can only be achieved by making use of every available means of attempting falsification.

6

Models in Application

INTRODUCTION

The authors of the MIT world models are guardedly optimistic about the applicability of their work. Forrester, for example, remarks, 'Having defined with care the model contained herein, and having examined its dynamic behaviour and implications, I have greater confidence in this world system model than in others that I now have available. Therefore, this is the model I should use for recommending actions'* (Preface to *World Dynamics*, Forrester, 1971a). In introducing his model, Meadows comments, 'We feel the model described here is already sufficiently developed to be of some use to decision makers' (*The Limits to Growth*, Meadows and coworkers, 1972). Meadows compares computer models with 'mental models based on a mixture of incomplete information and intuition that currently lies behind most political decisions'.

As has been pointed out elsewhere (Cole and coworkers, 1973), Forrester's model was based almost entirely on 'guessed' data and Meadows's, by his own reckoning, contained one-tenth of one per cent of the data required to make such a global model (see, for example, Encel and coworkers (1975)). Despite this, the implication is clearly that simulation models offer significant advantages over the current planning tools.

As we have seen, similar claims are commonly made by modellers and systems analysts. It is unfortunate that very often their expectations have not been realized. In this chapter we suggest several reasons why this has occurred. It is clear that one reason might be that often models simply do not forecast very well anyway. Another is that sophisticated modelling methods do not always fit readily into existing social and political institutions responsible for public policy.

Little has been written about the applicability to policy of world models. However, although we should be careful not to extract too much from the experiences of modellers in other areas (because, for global issues, there is relatively little comparable legislative organization and government and, possibly as a consequence, the propaganda element in a world modelling activity may be higher), it is enlightening to examine those experiences in a

*Reprinted with permission from *World Dynamics*, Second Edition by Jay W. Forrester, ©1973 Wright-Allen Press Inc. Cambridge, Mass. 02142, U.S.A.

number of subject areas in order to learn what would be needed if world models are to become serious aids to policy.

The discussion in this chapter will treat modelling subjects which are, in many respects, quite firmly based in the natural sciences, such as climate and agriculture, and more 'value laden' subjects such as urban systems and political conflict. These are hardly 'pure' disciplines in the sense of the somewhat artificial distinctions we have made for purpose of discussion in the previous sections. However, they are relevant to world models because of their complexity (as, for example, with meteorological systems) or their hybrid nature (as with urban systems). Nevertheless, the subject areas are sufficiently well established to have a recognizable title and a 'peer group' of practitioners.

In discussing the application of models, particular attention is paid to how well the various models forecast compared with other less sophisticated methods. As indicated earlier, we prefer to take a fairly pragmatic view of forecasting precision: that a forecast made for policy is accurate enough if making it more accurate would not demand a change in the inferences drawn from, or policies based on, the forecast. While this obviously is not sufficient even for all policy purposes, it is probably true that no forecasts yet reach this standard consistently.

To some extent, forecasting precision can be used to judge the current state of theory and modelling capability. The discussion, therefore, although not intended to provide an exhaustive review of modelling efforts in the areas discussed, gives some indication of the kind of standards of precision and application which modelling efforts currently achieve and which potentially global models ought to approach or exceed (if the 'holistic' argument is correct).

THE POLICY CONTEXT

All policy making is concerned with some assessment of the future, both in terms of the expected effect of policy and in terms of the likely context and environment in which future decisions will have to be made.

In general terms, the main reason for building and using models to assist policy making is that, if successful, they present a means of testing and exploring more rigorously and precisely the ramifications of policy without fear of costly mistakes in the real world where, in any case, the possibilities for experimentation are relatively limited.

Clearly, whether or not models will be successful in a given policy-making environment depends on whether they provide the right kind of information. To understand more precisely what kind of information might be needed, one must pay some attention to the character of policy itself. House (1973) has examined the meaning of policy with particular reference to the utility of models. He points out that an important characteristic of policy making is that it involves decision-taking at various levels and that the difference between the activities of these levels lies in the scope of the problems considered. This is an important feature of real-world decision making to bear in mind when assessing the relevance of models to policy.

With reference to what was said above, 'policy', with regard to global issues, is the establishment of a national level of guidelines which take account of global issues in such a way as to aid decision making on concrete issues in public affairs. Such guidelines are goal directed in that the objectives of government policy at a national level reflect, through the political process, some degree of agreement on the values, aspirations and interests of the various components of society, both in the short and longer term.

The difficulty of achieving this agreement has resulted in a process which is extremely diffuse. For example, not every public issue is decided in terms of articulated policy and, in fact, agreement on a given policy does not necessarily require agreement on its objectives. Policy decisions at all levels are directed towards some goal, but this may not be readily discernible from the decision itself. In practice, decision makers may prefer to make use of this ambiguity: the OECD (1972) remark as follows:

There is also the problem of the feasibility or the desirability of making policy objectives explicit. Societies are made up of groups with different interests and values, whose reactions to specific programmes often diverge. Thus, for electoral reasons, public decision-makers may prefer not to make too explicit policy objectives which may be detrimental—or felt to be detrimental—to one section of the community. And it is sometimes possible to achieve agreement on a specific programme amongst groups whose values and interests differ widely. Furthermore, given the rapidity of change and the uncertainty attached to it, public decision-makers often consider it preferable to leave open as many political options as possible, to avoid excessive commitment to one line of action, and to maintain the flexibility to deal with new problems and exploit new opportunities as they arise.

It is commonly accepted that public policy cannot be implemented successfully unless there is some overall public acceptance of the need for that policy, but the limitations on the influence of a high-level policy maker in his chain of command are greater than is often realized. Nelson (1974) has observed:

And it has become apparent to policy analysts concerned with budgeting, as it long has been apparent to administrators, that the chief problem of the central administrator is to pick and choose a limited number of places and situations for strategic intervention, rather than seriously trying to really 'steer the ship' in any detailed way.

Even for those cases where policy is deliberated and decided at a high level, it has become apparent that in many cases the steering wheel is but loosely connected to the rudder. The impact of policies depends in good part on the performance or reaction of people not under the direct control of the policy maker. In the first place, many of the problem activities or sectors are largely operated by private, not public, organisations, and the ways that public policy can influence what goes on are circumscribed and generally blunt.

The kind of complexity we have indicated here seems inevitable, given the nature of society, and thus it is clear that policy information needs cannot be simple or easy to satisfy, or even easy to define. This must be especially the case for policies with regard to global issues for which there is relatively little legislative organization and government.

In summary, the information needs of policy in general are affected by the following considerations:

(1) The hierarchical nature of the policy process throws up demands for information at different degrees of detail and precision.

(2) The multiplicity of factors to be accounted for requires that information should be in the simplest form, consistent with its being relevant and sufficient for the discussion.

(3) The often quite rapidly changing environment for policy or the emergence of new factors often brings a certain urgency to information demands.

(4) Finally, in view of the overall objective of policy, information has to be representative of all interest groups and issues involved.

Clearly, the relative importance of these information requirements depends on the circumstances, and they are clearly conflicting in terms of their demands. In attempting to build a model useful to policy, some compromise must inevitably be struck and an attempt made to take account in the model of as many of the above features as possible. In the following sections, we discuss the extent to which the nature of models, their performance and their institutional environment have made compromise between the different constraints on the use of models possible in a number of public policy areas. We are then in a position to draw some conclusions on the likely value of global models in policy making and the sort of circumstances in which we believe they may have something useful to offer.

MACRO-ECONOMIC MODELS

Lying at the heart of any global model is likely to be an economic model of some kind, if for no other reason than that much of the data available to researchers is couched in monetary or economic terms. No better parameter for 'trading-off' the relative value of different goods and services in a societal framework has yet been devised. Of course, economic models come in many forms and it is not our purpose to review them in any depth of detail here. For the obvious reason of being the most easily quantifiable, neoclassical economics shares with demography the honour of being the most rigorous of the social sciences. Furthermore, as we will see later, because of the relative success of economic models in the academic sense, they are also the most widely used social policy models.

The Economic Commission for Europe survey (United Nations, 1968) shows that most industrial countries employ a variety of macro-economic models for planning purposes. The survey notes that Eastern centrally-planned economies carry out medium-term planning on a larger scale than Western countries, where forecasting is mainly short-term. However, a number of countries are now considering long-term and short-term forecasts in areas related to economics, especially energy (Thomas, 1974).

Because of the importance of economic models, it is useful here to examine their degree of success as forecasting tools, since, in a sense, this sets the standard which currently might be a goal for global modellers. Two questions may be asked. How accurate are the models? How established are the underlying assumptions? In a recent volume, Ash and Smyth (1974) have reviewed the performance of three major short-term national economic models of the UK: those of the Treasury, the London Business School and the National Institute for Economic and Social Research. The review concludes that all the model forecasts are 'significantly more accurate than simply extrapolating or averaging past outcomes or assuming no change', i.e. are superior, in general, to forecasts based on naive extrapolation, smoothing or moving averages. A National Institute survey of its own forecasts shows that the performance has improved significantly since the early 1960s, but that continued improvement has resulted in additional complexity (Kennedy, 1969, cited by Ash and Smyth). Crawford (1974) compares the performance of the UK models for the period 1971–73 and finds an average error in the Spring forecast for the same year of about 1%, which he concludes is not intolerable, even though on a typical growth rate of 0–5% it represents a considerable error. Individual sectors or regional forecasts are usually much worse and it is with these that industrialists and planners are most often directly concerned.)

Ash and Smyth note, however, that despite the adoption of more sophisticated techniques, the performance of the Treasury model has not improved significantly in the last few years. They contrast this with the Dutch national model, which has improved, they believe, because of greater attention being paid to the 'dynamic structure' of economics. There may be other reasons for this relative improvement, e.g. that the Dutch economy is intrinsically less complex than that of the UK. In addition, an ECE survey (Council of Europe, 1973) indicates that, in order to calibrate the model, many of the relationships were linearized. This report also comments that very often models were deliberately kept 'simple' because of the poor quality of the available data, and because planners are not sufficiently experienced to apply successfully more complex methods.

In the main, it is not actual model results which are published, but interpretations of the results, in the light of 'judgement'. It is interesting and significant (as described in a recent *Business Week* article, June 29th, 1974) that, over the last year, with so many disturbing factors in the world and national economies, the 'seat-of-the-pants' forecasters (who rely entirely on judgement) have had a better record than the mathematical modellers. Judgemental forecasters rely mainly on a set of leading indicators of economies and, despite the recent variability of the evidence, a greater reliance on experience and intuition does seem to have been more flexible (and successful) than the more sophisticated models. The American Statistical Association publishes a list of projections by a selection of US economic forecasters, using a range of techniques. There is a fair spread of forecasts; for example, the unweighted mean of eight forecasts of US real growth for 1974 was about 1%, with a standard deviation of about 1%, indicating errors of around 100% on the predicted figure). When the forecasts were revised (in the light of the oil crisis etc.), the new average was zero growth with about 0.5% standard deviation. Without reading too much into these figures, it is clear that there must be a fair degree of consensus between the assumptions of the forecasters, but also, from the point of view of making decisions based on the forecasts, that there is a relatively high degree of variation. One more point worth mentioning is (as Ash and Smyth show) that endogenous variables tend, in normal circumstances, to be forecast more accurately than exogenous variables (such as foreign demand), which were usually estimated by judgement. This seems to indicate again that models can provide extra precision over simple methods, and indeed many modellers are attempting to include a greater number of nominally exogenous variables into national economic models.

However, the complexity of economic models, and some difficulties caused by them, should not be underestimated. To quote Ball (1967):

As facilities for handling larger models have become available, there has been some tendency to consider models of increasingly large size. The major example of this is the SSRC–Brookings model, developed by a substantial team of econometricians in the US ... In its full form, this model of the US economy runs to something between 300 and 400 relations. Size in itself is of course no virtue, and the increase in system size brings with it both intellectual and organizational problems. It is a major activity to establish the behaviour of systems of this size, and in particular to discover where the system goes wrong. There are also considerable problems of system evaluation, for it cannot be decided how good your system is without specifying your objective. Typically, in large systems, some variables are predicted or simulated well and others badly.

If one compares the kind of criticisms made of global models of Forrester and Meadows with those of standard economic accounting devices such as the Leontief input–output matrix formulation, one finds many defects in common. For example, in both methods, functional forms are arbitrary and are highly aggregated. However, it has to be emphasized that these defects are less serious in a short-term model, especially a *calibrated* model (since parameter values can adjust to compensate for irregularities in relationships), than in a long-term global model. Nevertheless, wide-ranging and inconclusive debates, for example on the causes of inflation or the 'best' model for development, expose serious deficiencies in our understanding of socio-economic processes.

A critical reason for the success of economic models relative to many other kinds of social model may be noted. Kaldor (1970) points out that post-war governments in the UK have consistently come to judge economic performance in quantitative terms and that this has led to a 'managerial' approach to government handling of the economy. Government success is now largely measured by its ability to achieve reasonable targets for the four basic economic indicators—employment level, balance of payments, growth and inflation.

The existence of a managerial environment with relatively few objectives, more or less clearly stated, is almost the precursor of a successful policy model and may go some way to explaining the usefulness of the Treasury models. It is also at the root of much of the criticism of the systems analytic approach to policy formation. Such a clear statement of goals does not usually hold for other social situations over this length of time. It is also possible that, as Schultze (1968) has suggested, the political–economic process has itself been modified to some extent by the adoption of new analytic methods, and we will return to this point later.

Even though there is often disagreement between the projections obtained from the different economic models for a given country, it is generally considered that such models are of some value for policy making. In any case, the existence of economic models outside government provides a useful check for Treasury forecasts, as does public academic discussion about the assumptions and methods used in the model. General agreement on which economic indicators are of interest is an important factor which enables the forecasts of different models to be compared. For example, in the case of the UK, quarterly forecasts of the National Institute for Economic and Social Research and the London Business School are published and available for comparison with the Treasury models. Additionally, personnel are exchanged regularly between the teams working on these models and between these teams and others. It is interesting that the National Institute's forecasting role was originally established in response to a request from the Economic Advisor to the Treasury in order to provide an alternative set of forecasts to those of the Treasury itself, from an outside and independent observer.

Of course, short-term national economic models as a whole are certainly not without their critics and it is significant that Ash and Smyth, following their analysis of UK experience, are obliged to make the point that economic forecasting is not a 'waste of time'. On the whole, criticisms against economic modellers do not seem to have been as vitriolic as those against other analysts. However, the 'compliance' we have suggested should not be taken to indicate that there is universal consensus amongst economists concerning even a single economy.

An important reason for the relative success of economic models is that they are constructed with the assumption of a relatively stable social environment within the value framework of the major political parties and permanent officials. In discussing the 'Policy relevance of models in world politics', Tanter (1972) remarks as follows:

In any discussion of policy relevance several criteria are usually implicit. One criterion states that a model must be acceptable or compatible with the dominant value framework of the policy maker. Value, ethical, and moral considerations define the range within which policy influencers can operate. Unless a model falls within this range, it cannot hope to be policy relevant. Models which allow for a greater number of alternatives within this range are more policy relevant.*

In this respect there is a sharp contrast between the situation for economic and global models. Because of this consensus, the models used by Treasury

*This excerpt from 'The Policy Relevance of Models in World Politics' by Raymond Tanter is reprinted from Journal of Conflict Resolution, vol. XVI, no. 4 (Dec. 1972) p. 561 by permission of the Publisher, Sage Publications Inc. (Beverly Hills, Calif. and London).

officials do not change with the changes in Government, although, of course, the 'questions asked' of the models do. This provides a firm research environment closely intertwined with current policy issues and permits the models to be systematically updated as new information or theories become available. Even so, as we pointed out earlier, in situations such as the present, when there is considerable uncertainty as to the underlying mechanisms causing inflation and variations in a host of other economic indicators, the ability of economists and modellers to keep pace with events fails and the quality of forecasts falls behind. These anomalies are not easily corrected; one review based on interviews with many of the leading US economists concluded that the fundamental problem being that the theoretical base on which economic forecasts are made is inadequate, and advances are urgently needed (*Business Week*, June 29, 1974).

Thus, the situation for macro-economic models may be summarized as follows: Most governments now employ models of varying complexity for short-term economic planning. The useful predictive power of the models is restricted to a few quarters ahead, even though they are based on good data for at least the past decade. Because they are usually fairly complex, the models are assessed through strong peer group activity mainly on their 'track record', i.e. their proven useful forecasting ability. The relatively solid data base and the possibility of testing their predictive performance is in contrast with that for long-term global models. Economists do not disagree that these models are far from satisfactory; however, they would often comply with much of the underlying structure and assumptions. This is less true of models of global economic development. If a similar consensus is ever reached for global models, they may occupy a similar place to these economic models in relation to government and international policy.

ECOLOGICAL MODELS

If one neglects for the moment man-made disturbances due to the emission of waste heat or particulates into the atmosphere, models of climatic systems provide a good demonstration of the present state-of-the-art in modelling complex 'physical' dynamic systems. The greatest successes in this area appear to be in predicting 'micro' events such as the growth of *individual* clouds, rather than in the evolution of total weather patterns. Nevertheless, some models have simulated some aspects of regional weather patterns rather well. There are, of course, severe difficulties in obtaining sufficiently precise measurements of the relevant parameters in a weather system; and indeed best parameterization is still a matter of debate.

The atmosphere is a dynamic system, continually dispersing and disposing of pollution, and the effects of individual pollutants are highly interrelated. Thus, for example, to construct a model to examine the effects of waste heat alone can only be a preliminary exercise. 'Back of envelope' calculations indicate that local and regional temperature variations due to waste heat from industrial and urban agglomeration may give rise to distortion of established weather patterns. Peterson (1973) considers that the first steps towards building models capable of approaching these problems have been made. However, at present, there is still dispute as to whether man's activities are causing an increase in average global temperatures (from waste heat emission) or a decrease (through pollutants breaking down the insulating ozone layer). Fears of a heat death and of a man-induced ice age have both been expressed.

Day-to-day predictions using the rather sophisticated weather models which are used by most national meteorological offices are now better than the 'naive' assumption that tomorrow's weather will be very much like today's.

Miyakoda (1974) describes tests made on a United States National Oceanic and Atmospheric Administration model which involve calculation of the correlation coefficient between actual and predicted deviations of pressure from monthly normals; it was found that the coefficient decreased monotonically from unity initially to zero on the eleventh day, implying a recognized predictive capability up to the tenth day. Rain represents the most difficult element to predict; the above model has only proved useful for up to four days, and even for this is restricted to predictions of large-scale rain patterns covering an area of several hundred square kilometres.

Meteorological prediction can be expected to improve as data, theory and computer techniques advance. The computer forecasts are based on rather well known 'first principle' calculations from hydrodynamic and thermodynamic theory; the main constraints on prediction arise from the complex features of the system such as the interaction of the atmosphere with the oceans and the importance of 'micro' processes such as turbulence. Experiments suggest that a hemispherical model has an inherent practical limit of ten days forecasting, while that of global models (which are now being introduced) is about three weeks. The existence of this limit stems from the fact that the atmosphere can never be observed perfectly, but improvements in data collection should allow the limit to be approached.

In the analysis of biological processes, especially those concerned with food chains and the interrelationships between species, the systems approach has gained increasing merit. The work of Odum (1972) on nutrient flows appears to have been particularly useful. Maynard Smith (1974) has recently reviewed progress in ecological modelling and his conclusions indicate the experimental nature of much of this research at the present time. It is quite clear that, to achieve a fair understanding of particular ecosystem behaviour, a sound analysis of its components is needed. However, the specificity of each locale is often such as to make a high degree of generalization at a global or regional level inappropriate.

Writing of the problems of modelling river estuaries, Howells (1973) concludes that, although much progress has been made in recent years, and while models are useful research tools, more data of the right kind is required before realistic prediction is possible.

Although many micro-processes in a limited range of species are well understood under laboratory conditions, there are many defects in the understanding of ecological systems as a whole. The problems of data collection are clearly immense and even attempts such as that of Jansson (1972) to construct an operational species model of the Baltic, sufficient to estimate the long-term effect of the industrial and agricultural pollutants, pale when compared with the problems of building a global eco-model. By comparison, the commodity projections of FAO (1967) and OECD (1969) are more traditional. The FAO uses income elasticities to estimate future demand for various commodities, given assumptions regarding per-capita income. United Nations population projections are used. The FAO generally assume constant prices, while the OECD forecast the production 'likely to arise from the continuation of recent trends' regarding policies and prices; supply and demand are treated independently, with the exception of certain livestock products. It might be expected that these projections will certainly be no better than their constituent economic forecasts, even neglecting the complications of forecasting arising from climatic variations.

In meteorology and oceanography, theoretical and technical problems achieve a fair degree of international consensus. The issues are multinational and, as a rule, not divisive, so there would seem to be some possibilities for international cooperation in this field. Difficulties are most likely to arise over apportioning responsibility for policy implementation with regard to airborne or seaborne pollutants. International learned societies and institutions play an important role in resolving such conflicts and spearheading the introduction of a united global attack on environmental problems. Agreement between members of the international scientific community in contact with their own national governments provides some common technical basis for discussion. A similar role might be envisaged for more general global models.

As an example of the international collaboration which has been possible on this type of study, the International Ocean Institute was established in 1972, in cooperation with the United Nations Development Programme. Projects on the Mediterranean, the Caribbean, the Arctic and the Pacific, which are designed to contribute to the definition of an 'economic–ecological infrastructure' upon which a legal ocean regime could be based, are under way. This can clearly clarify concepts for the U.N. Conference on the Law of the Sea (Borgesse, 1973).

A similar project, which depends much more heavily on a dynamic model, involves the cooperation of several Baltic countries, for whom a coming together over this common issue at a political level is difficult:

The construction of these models and the coupling of them to a predictable macro-model for the whole Baltic Sea requires a close co-operation between all Baltic nations. Within some fields a close co-operation already exists. The Baltic Oceanographers, an informed association of scientists, regardless of nationality and political thinking, has worked well for several years. They have used the same methods and arranged regular meetings. (Jansson, 1972).

DEMOGRAPHIC MODELS

Since, indirectly, many world problems are considered to arise from 'population growth', proper treatment of population within a global model is impera- tive. As we have indicated, there is little consensus yet as to the best way to do this. Page (1973) has reviewed the history of official population forecasting since the time of Malthus and concludes that methods have improved only margi- nally. Recent forecasts of the UK population over the last twenty years have shifted erratically, with predicted increases of from five to fifteen millions over the present figure by the year 2000. The UK Commission on Population consi- dered a wide range of possible forecasts, based on a large modelling exercise. Despite this the actual population 20 years later was outside the range considered.

The variations are clearly closely tied to fluctuating perceptions of economic fortunes and possibly also to the impact of statements such as those contained in *The Limits to Growth*. However, precise quantification seems to be especially difficult, although the Bariloche team claim to have built a good 'explanatory' regression model of life expectancy compared across nations. Most advances seem to have come from a more careful selection of data and more detailed analysis, e.g. taking explicit account of the number of women of childbearing age. The World 3 model contained a rather elaborate population sub-model, which represented an attempt to identify and include several of the causal mechanisms underlying fecundity and mortality levels. Hyrenius, at the 1974 World Population Conference, suggested that an accurate model would only be achieved through continued elaboration and sophistication (including further disaggregation and calibration) of the Meadows type of approach. In the Mesarovic–Pestel model, populations are divided into yearly cohorts on a world regional basis. Given the difficulty in establishing causal relationships in other than a general way, and given the poorness of much data, such attention to modelling detail may be premature.

A group at the United Nations International Labour Office are constructing a population and employment model as part of the Population and Employ- ment project of the World Employment Programme. In this model population is divided into five-year age groups except for the youngest and oldest groups, which are respectively considered in more and less detail. The team have used survey data to calibrate their first application (to the Philippines, Wéry and coworkers (1974)) and have succeeded in provoking a dialogue of critical debate between the model builders and the country concerned. Other appli- cations to Brazil, Kenya and Yugoslavia are under way with ILO teams work- ing inside the countries concerned. The model is not intended to provide predictions of population growth, but to examine economic and demographic policies and their likely impacts. The model is unusual in that it examines both the effects of population growth on economic factors and vice versa.

POLITICAL CONFLICT MODELS

Political processes represent the most 'value laden' aspect of international developments and the extent to which political events should or could be for- mally integrated into a global model is also a matter of debate among modellers.

In the Meadows model, political interactions were included as part of the general trend of industrial and demographic development. In models composed of several regions, political events may be treated as micro-processes subsumed into assumptions about trade, capital and aid flows. The Mesarovic–Pestel study has policy variables which are explicitly left open to adjustment by 'policy makers and politicians' from the different world regions. It is fair to say that, to date, attempts to make explicit numerical models of political decisions have had little success; models of strategic choices too have often been misleading because, among other things, of a misunderstanding of the cultural and value basis of one's 'opponents' and because of the difficulty of quantifying value choices. Tanter (1972) has analysed a wide range of conflict policy models and shows that the 'predictions' of very few have been used to explain past events in an attempt to validate the model. McClelland and coworkers' (1971) work, however, is an exception; and it is just possible to show that a 'limited reciprocal response' theory is a better predictor of US–Soviet policy than a random or perfect reciprocal theory. If this represents the current limits of achievement in this area, it follows that there is probably only limited benefit to be derived from including such results explicitly into a globally disaggregated long-range forecasting model and that investigating a variety of possible 'scenarios' may be more appropriate.

URBAN AND GEOGRAPHIC MODELS

Urban models provide a microcosm of many of the problems and issues facing world modellers since they attempt to combine technological, economic and social variables, and a fair amount of attention will be paid here to their recent fortunes. Urban models, attempting to explain urban structure in classical economic terms, date back to von Thunen in the early nineteenth century. However, as early as 1858, Carey noted the analogy of urbanization to the gravity model of physics; Lowry (1964) used this social physics model to describe industrial growth. In fact, the model provides a moderately good representation of behaviour, although its empirical base provides no attempt to explain the mechanisms underlying that behaviour, the reverse situation to micro-economic utility models. Wilson (1970) has more recently extended the gravity model to account for statistical and information theories and Sayer (1974) has extended the model to dynamic formulation. In the main, however, most dynamic models have been simulation models, such as Forrester's *Urban Dynamics* model.

Lee (1973) finds that during the 1960s, goals held out for models tended to change in the light of performance deficiencies. Certainly, bold claims have been made for the success of some of the large-scale models. For example, of the San Francisco Housing model, Little (1966) (cited by Lee, 1973) considered that early runs confirmed the value of a model as a means of representing a complex system and indicated that the model was a valuable aid for testing the effects of major policies.

Lee says of this model:

The estimates of housing construction produced by these runs fit actual data in an intuitively satisfactory way. One entry was substantially off, but five of the six marginal totals differed from the actual by ten per cent or less, and the two-period total was only three per cent off. Later, additional data became available, including new data and more detail. Testing the model against the new data showed that previous conformance on totals had been achieved at the expense of large compensating errors in sub-categories, and that even a careful adjustment of the parameters left some major categories at well over a hundred per cent error ... One of the extreme cases was in luxury apartments, in which the model predicted 1092 new units in a two year period, while the market produced only 64. (Lee, 1973)*.

However, specific urban models have rarely been subjected to a critical assessment. Brewer and Hall (1973) note that the only model in the USA to have received detailed outside appraisal was Forrester's *Urban Dynamics* model. Even so, the spectrum of views expressed by critics was so wide as to make any kind of definitive evaluation impossible.

It is now widely accepted that the large-scale land-transport models, which were in vogue during the 1960s and are comparable to global models in terms of complexity and the mix of factors they contain, have been largely unsuccessful. The main reasons for this seem to have been inadequate theory and a level of complexity which made the models unsuited to their policy environment.

World modellers face a rather similar problem in terms of model construction, and clearly there is a danger of falling into the same traps. The issues are complex, and the danger is the possibility of creating even greater complexity by attempting to over-generalize.

Most authors who have reviewed the progress of urban models recently, including Lee (1973), Brewer and Hall (1973) and Sears (1973), advocate that efforts should be directed at building more manageable models. A few authors (for example, Kajona, 1973) advocate a high level of disaggregation because, without this (they say), the necessary relevance to policy issues cannot be achieved. Clearly they may have a point here, but it may not be possible to achieve this at the present state of theory and technical capability. Obviously, there is a need not only to continue experimentation but also to learn from the mistakes of the past.

From his analysis of land use models, Lee concludes:

These models were begun in the early 1960s and largely abandoned by the end of the 1960s. Considerable effort was expended on them, and a good deal was learned. Contrary to what has often been claimed, what was learned had almost nothing to do with urban spatial structure; the knowledge that was increased was our understanding of model building and its relationship to policy analysis. For that alone, it was a valuable experience, but not if the lessons are ignored. For many in planning and many in a number of related fields that have recently become interested in planning problems, the lessons are being ignored ... The models were designed to replicate too complex a system in a single shot, and they were expected to serve too many purposes at the same time.*

*Reprinted by permission of the Journal of the American Institute of Planners, Vol. 39, no. 3, May 1973.

As we have indicated earlier, another reason for avoiding too much complexity at the present time arises from institutional factors. Modellers claim that the explicit representation of ideas in the form of a computer model can improve communication between researchers, policy makers and the public. It may be that in the case of *The Limits to Growth*, this aspect was overemphasized or even abused. As the OECD (1972) observe, the onus is very much on the modeller to ensure that this communication is achieved:

The real complexity of the problems under consideration—often compounded by the apparent complexity of the analytical methods used—can be an obstacle to a real dialogue between the policy maker and the analyst, unless the former is willing to make some effort to understand, and the latter to make a similar effort to present the results of their analysis in a form that is comprehensible to the non-specialist.

Some experienced urban modellers have adopted a quite different approach, by attempting to work in much closer contact with practising planners (Broadbent, 1973; Massey and Cordey-Hayes, 1971; Barras and coworkers, 1971). In the main, they find that only the simplest techniques seem to be of real value. Even this arrangement has its problems and, as Broadbent points out, having introduced the models, satisfactory data requirements again present the major stumbling block.

His conclusions from these exercises again begin to show up methodological problems. Lack of data often means that the interpretation of output becomes the major feature of the study, and consequently that presentation of output and user-orientation become more important than specific model formulation. Indeed, in general, the models which are used more or less regularly and are comprehensible to urban planners are the simple empirical 'gravity' models, which are used to estimate trip densities and retailing potential, and the even more straightforward input/output framework. Simple models more or less conforming to the latter structure and with few, or sometimes no, calibrated parameters are apparently used by some local authorities (e.g. Sharpe and Brotchie, 1973). Often these are coupled to linear programming systems in an effort to produce 'optimal solutions' to particular planning problems. Inevitably, such solutions are sub-optimal in the sense that intangibles cannot be accounted for satisfactorily. Despite this, for certain issues, the optimal solution may be fairly close to the 'best' solution selected by the 'seat of the pants' planners. Of course, in such cases a model is not being used as a forecasting tool, but rather as an accounting framework to demonstrate the equilibrium result of particular planning decisions (and in terms of our definition, the models are static rather than dynamic).

Even though these models are used, it would be wrong to assume that they are considered entirely satisfactory. However, it is unlikely that much progress can be made without the emergence of better theory. Despite this, the results of such models are often the basis of discussion at public inquiries and criticism tends to be directed at the antiquity of the data base rather than at the model itself. In view of the large data base for urban models, the opportunity for extensive model verification does exist, a situation very different from that for global models. The rather long time required for their construction is often not available in the typical planning department, and consequently they do not find the stable environment afforded the national economic models. There are, however, exceptions to this: some transportation models are now relied upon and are functioning well.

Sometimes, where models have been total failures, other explanations can be found, such as the internal 'politics' of the planning department or the excessive zeal of the analysts employed. The (now defunct) San Francisco model, which Lee (1973) estimates as probably costing $500,000, was likely 'to take another $250,000 to get the already working housing model into shape for potential usage'. Brewer (1973) have taken a close look at the reasons for the construction of the San Francisco model and from his analysis one thing seems clear: that the building of an effective planning tool was not the major objective of many of the major parties involved!

The extent to which urban models have been a 'disaster' is currently a matter of widespread dispute, occupying considerable space in leading town planning journals (see, for example, the *Journal of the American Institute of Planners* and *The Planner* for the second half of 1973). One problem is certainly that modellers have claimed too much for their products, which has led to a strong reaction on many occasions. For example, Cherrington, then Assistant Secretary for Transportation in the US Government, admonished systems analysts and modellers as follows (cited by OECD, 1972):

In the first instance, it strikes me that there is considerable over-reaching in this field, perhaps wider and bigger claims than the state of the art can in fact deliver ... For example, there are a good many late contracts, a good many overrun contracts and a good many contracts which end up with little more than junk. The situation is not yet fatal to the further willingness of the government, including the Department of Transportation, to support efforts in this area, but it could easily get to that point; and to be frank, we are not very sophisticated in selecting between the good guys and the charlatans.

I would urge you to give some attention to the utility and use of the models and studies which you are developing and somewhat less to the advanced methodologies and mathematical niceties of the models ... If you want your products to be used and if you want to be supported so that you can do a certain amount of methodological research, I think you must pay more attention, than has been true in the past, to the utility of your work in the planning process.

This last remark, we believe, is critical, and applicable to modellers in other areas.

PROGRAMME POLICY BUDGETING SYSTEM, COST BENEFIT ANALYSIS, ETC.

In the main, the methods used in central government policy have not included dynamic simulation models. However, methods such as Cost Benefit Analysis and Programme Policy Budgeting System (PPBS) have been used in various ways for more than a decade. They involve many of the same conceptual difficulties of quantification and analysis and have been rather thoroughly investigated by a number of critics. It is therefore pertinent to record experience with them here. Pavitt (1972) concludes his analysis of analytic techniques in government science policy with the following comparatively conciliatory remark:

While one can argue probably that the use of formal analytical techniques can lead to better decisions, one can equally argue that they can lead to worse decisions. Strong doses of caution and humility are needed when beginning to use them. Trying to be very ambitious too early can be disastrous. This is what happened with the introduction of the PPB System into the US Government. And recent empirical investigations have shown that both technological forecasting and long-range planning activities in industry are sometimes no more than in-grown paper exercises with little or no influence on either policy-making or operations.

In this comment, one can see many of the criticisms made against urban and other modellers. Overclaiming is commonplace, as Hoos (1972) notes after her detailed case studies of four expensive and time consuming systems analyses carried out by corporations for government. She remarks that 'the organisations taking on governmental contracts were somewhat pretentious'.

Pavitt (1972) also cites Lindblom (1959) and others in casting doubt upon the effectiveness of these techniques, even in the military and industrial fields:

For example, it has often been claimed that formal, analytical techniques have been most successfully used in the military sector, where the social constraints on technological developments are minimal. But while these techniques have been useful in making choices among proven weapon-systems, their value in the planning of military technological development has been much more questionable. Recently, the US Deputy Defense Secretary, Mr. David Packard argued, that one of the major causes of cost over-runs in the development of weapon-systems has been the commitment of major resources before technological problems have been overcome, and he has advocated greater reliance on prototype developments rather than 'paper studies' as a guide to decisions on which weapons to bring into operational use.

(When economic and social factors obtrude in decisions on whether to develop or use a new piece of technology, our ability to forecast is similarly limited. In civilian industry, two empirical studies have shown no correlation between *ex ante* evaluations of R & D projects and *ex post* real performance. And other studies have shown the difficulties of predicting the market's reaction to new technology.)

Hoos finds that many analysts were unaware of the arbitrariness and falseness of many of their own assumptions. Studies were oriented towards a certain discipline and often unaware of alternative paradigms and theories. Also, total unawareness was shown of the social context of the work, which often began with the premise that a rigid hierarchical management structure existed to carry out their recommendations. In this, analysts assumed central administrative processes and overlooked the existence of legal, constitutional and social constraints, and the interests of other government departments. Thus major factors were ignored. From a technical modelling point of view, the data which were 'admitted' (to use the definition we adopted in Chapter 5) were chosen to support the bias rather than to enlighten. Added to this, some reports examined were not even internally consistent, so that even the claim that the methods provided rigour was not justified. This kind of criticism would be less deserved had the costs of analysis not been so large and had the interests of many more conscientious researchers not been damaged by the actions of less scrupulous colleagues.

We conclude this section by repeating the remark of Schultze (1968) who, as Director of the Bureau of the Budget under President Johnson, was in part responsible for the introduction of PPBS into US Government: 'If PPB[S] is to survive as a system, it must fit into the political process and at the same time must modify that process'.*

The remark is important for two reasons. It suggests once again that analysts have failed to appreciate the context of their policies, and also that the systems approach to public policy must be viewed as any other 'technology'. It can have both positive and deleterious effects. What critics such as Pavitt and Hoos have argued is that the positive achievements have been small; what the 'anti-technocrats' such as Armytage (1965) have warned against is the widespread adoption of the 'management' philosophy. This, as Schultze implies, might be the inevitable concomitant of the successful implementation of systems methods in social policy and, as we discussed earlier, does seem to have been the case with national economic models.

THE ROLE OF MODELS IN POLICY

In terms of the categorization of models as 'policy', 'viewpoint' and 'experimental' provided in Chapter 3, it is seen that relatively few models can truly be considered as policy models. However, the most successful economic and industrial models and models of a largely 'physical' character such as meteorological models appear to qualify since they are often accepted by a fair spectrum of opinions. Economic development models, conflict models and most urban models tend more often to fall into the category of viewpoint models although many (including the MIT global models) are really experimental models which, for one reason or another, gain a great deal of publicity. In practice, it has often been the case that the policy issues examined using analytic methods have been so complex that the methods have been unable to contribute greatly. But, as we have seen, there are exceptions to this. Although it would be dangerous to extrapolate too loosely from experiences at, say, the local or tactical level to the wider strategic level at which global models would be expected to find a use, there are a number of generalizations that can be made.

There has been a tendency to attempt too much with a single model. Consequently, even the apparently reasonable claim that formally structuring a problem leads to clarification has often turned out not to be true in practice simply because of extraneous detail. In the main, attempts to produce 'general

*Reproduced from 'The Politics and Economics of Public Spending' by Charles L. Schultze. © 1968 by Brookings Institution, Washington, D.C.

purpose' models accounting for a large number of issues or interest groups have led to models which are at the same time simplistic, in the sense that many of the relationships appear naive and factors of possibly great importance are omitted, and complex, in that the detailed behaviour of the model is seldom completely understood by the modeller, let alone by the policy maker. Even so, a survey in the US showed that 'large' models were not necessarily used less than small models (NSF, 1974), but indicated that this could be due to the bias of the sample (many of the smaller models are constructed by students who consider them to be relevant to policy).

Thus, while a 'holistic' model may not be complex enough to represent adequately the real problems under consideration, its general opaqueness is likely to be a severe handicap in application. According to Pavitt (1972), complex analytic methods on top of the complexities of policy decisions lead to the following:

Mutual incomprehension between the policy-maker and the analyst. The former may not understand the latter's language (especially if it is dressed up in pseudoscientific jargon), and the latter may not understand—or even be aware of—the essential features of the political process;
Mutual distrust between the analyst and the scientific and engineering community, when the analyst ignores the specific characteristics of scientific and technological activities (e.g. uncertainty, long term horizons); and the scientific and engineering community refuses or resents explaining to the analyst what these characteristics are;
Lack of explicitness in any analysis about assumptions which may be technically shaky, or which may hide political value judgements. Sometimes this may be done intentionally by the analyst or the policy-maker. But given the type of training and the intellectual apparatus that many analysts have, it may also result from a propensity to concentrate on quantifiable factors and methodological refinements, to the neglect of often important 'intangible' factors.

The essential complexity of models attempting to represent a wide spectrum of issues leads to a lack of manageability which manifests itself in a number of other ways. Large models are slow to develop; if they are to be successful, they require a good basis of theory and data, normally only achieved over a considerable period of time. As a result, it is often difficult for them to provide the degree of flexibility required in a rapidly changing policy environment. The importance of this has been emphasized since the 1973 Arab–Israeli war and the action of the OPEC countries which followed; any model which included wide-ranging social, political or economic factors had to be capable of either forecasting or incorporating the repercussions of the restrictions in oil supplies and price increases (Cole, 1974). With other commodity producers discussing the possibility of similar cartel action, it seems likely that, in the future, discontinuities will play an increasingly important role.

The time required to construct and test a model may also be such that the problem it represents has become more difficult to solve or has 'disappeared'. According to Schultze (1968) it turns out that simply because this time has elapsed interest groups have come into being with entrenched positions which often tend to frustrate compromise. These factors must reduce the confidence in such models of policy makers who are used to 'driving by the seat of their pants' (Jeffers, 1973). In any case, Lindblom (1959) and Lindblom and Hirshman (1962) have argued that empirical and 'incremental' methods of decision making are not only the most widely practised, but also the most efficient, for the types of activities for which governments are responsible.

The question of confidence is important before a policy maker will use a model. As Tanter (1972) has observed, the policy maker must first have confidence in the assumptions of the model, i.e. they must reflect his own point of veiw, at least in part, and secondly he must have confidence in the way the model manipulates those assumptions. The first is difficult in any kind of 'general purpose' model and the second is made more difficult if the manipulations are obscured by over-complexity. The apparent rationality and objectivity of such models can hide quite dubious assumptions concerning the measurability of parameters or can imply a consensus of views which does not exist.

The question of the confidence of the public is also very important. The impenetrability of computer models may constrain debate about their underlying assumptions, and it can be argued that they inhibit the democratic process. As discussed in Chapter 1, the 'systems' approach has become increasingly attractive to some people and its ultimate goal is perhaps, as suggested by Ramo (1969), the realization of a 'golden age [where] people are wedded to creative logic and objectivity to get solutions to society's problems'. However, it is hard to believe that the general public would be happy with what Weinberg (1969) has seen as 'cheap technological fixes which will short-cut the solution of social problems without having first to solve the infinitely more difficult problem of strongly motivating people'. The least desirable situation of all is perhaps that described by Sinclair (1973): 'In the current dearth of scientific knowledge of the future and of a limit to what can be known, there lies a danger which must be avoided at all cost; that is the attachment of spurious certainty to predictions of tenuous truthfulness'.

The argument that models represent a more explicit structure for policy formation than that currently used is, as we have suggested, suspect, because they can scarcely be called explicit by those not versed in the mathematical language in which they are couched, so decision makers may have some fear that modellers are attempting to usurp their role, and also because policy makers may wish to make use of ambiguity with respect to the goals on which their strategies are based. While it could be argued that these are deficiencies in society rather than in models, it is clear that many modellers have not appreciated their importance when advocating their products. Analysis of a recent US survey (NSF, 1974) suggested that although the extent of model use is hard to measure, 'the most generous estimate [itself based on the information of researchers building the models] would be that more than a third of those models intending policy use fail to achieve it, while a conservative estimate could put the failure rate as high as two thirds'. This is particularly unfortunate since, as House and Tyndall (1973) remark, 'If one were to attend a number of the professional meetings held each year or read the articles written by practitioners of the modelling art, it would become apparent that almost all feel that their creations are "policy" models'.

Lee (1972) suggests a solution which corresponds closely to Tanter's (1972) conclusion that, if modellers want to influence policy, they must first find a political figure sympathetic to their views. Lee suggests further that modellers require a 'judicious' amount of evidence to support their case and 'some astute marketing based on our knowledge of the experience and perceptions of existing policy makers'. This approach clearly recognizes the position of the modeller as a legitimate contributor to the political process but also that, in general, one model cannot hope to accommodate successfully the necessary spectrum of opinions and concerns.

Ash and Smyth (1974) make the Machiavellian suggestion that there are circumstances in which the best forecasts are not always the most useful. They point out that government offices can anticipate the response of public and private authorities to their forecasts, and that, for example, demand management can be achieved by 'judiciously misleading the private sector'. Governments could, in principle, express desired targets rather than objective assessments of future developments in its forecasts in order to influence behaviour.

Of course Ash and Smyth are not arguing against the need for better and more accurate forecasting methods. Moreover, a forecast should not be treated in the abstract; its role as an active agent causing changes within society should also be taken into consideration. Whether their observation is the right approach is a matter of opinion. However, the possibility of 'self-fulfilling' forecasts suggests that the practice of disturbing predictions may not be entirely unethical. 'Overemphasis' of certain issues was considered by many people to be legitimate in the case of *The Limits to Growth* model.

RESEARCHERS, SPONSORS AND THEIR VALUES

It may seem that what has been said so far in this chapter applies only to models to be used in a government setting, for example within a ministry or local planning office. This is not implied, since very much the same criteria are often relevant for university based research. Especially in the social sciences, researchers are likely to want to influence government policy. Clearly, a desire to play the advocate's role requires the same credibility in his research model although, of course, other non-governmental and less direct channels are open to the university researchers for the presentation of their work.

What is the 'correct' relationship between university researchers and policy? The traditional view characterized by Flexner (1930) still prevails to a great extent. He advocated that 'scientists should not incur responsibilities for policies' and that the 'social scientists must be divorced from the conduct of politics'. Even if this is a researcher's wish—which we consider unlikely to be true in most cases—it is difficult to see how, in fields where beliefs and values cannot be eliminated, researchers can divorce themselves from expressions which are to some degree political.

The conflict between academic rigour and political or personal predispositions becomes especially acute when one is dealing with such ill-defined and under-researched areas as those considered by world modellers. For example, although it is now fairly widely felt that the technical and theoretical content of the MIT models is quite unsatisfactory, it is also true that the modellers and their sponsors, the Club of Rome, were at least at the outset of their work, convinced of the seriousness and urgency of the issues they publicized.

The Club of Rome and the 'Limits to growth' team started their study apparently with the conviction that the 'World problematique' was near crisis point; understandably this raised the question of what means of propagating their concern were justified and appropriate. In a recent article 'The moment of truth is approaching', Aurelio Peccei, the founder of the Club, repeats the urgency he perceives in mankind's predicament and puts forward the Club of Rome's justification for the dramatic presentation of the 'Limits to growth' exercise and especially the use of an elaborate computer model to draw attention to the Club's views (Peccei, 1973b).

He explains that, having previously failed by more conventional methods to shake people out of their faith in the ability of technology to overcome future crises, 'the club felt that probably nothing short of shock treatment could do the job'. The immediate purpose of the club was to:

search for a device capable of opening a breach in the hearts and minds of people, of arousing their awareness to the complexity and seriousness of the world problematique. After long consideration, a commando operation was decided upon, in the hope that its tactical success might have strategic consequences.

Thus the high-powered campaign we have alluded to in the Introduction was set in operation.

Peccei (1973a) reports that:

Reactions to the book have been remarkable both in the United States and Europe, and indicate that, despite criticisms of its scientific accuracy and even its basic validity, it confirms the qualitative and intuitive conclusions of many. Many government departments and international organisations ... literally hundreds of conferences and seminars ... parliamentary questions, multinational corporations ... even a matter of controversy between members of the commission of the European Communities.

The 'success' of *The Limits to Growth* experiment can, to a large extent, be attributed to the use of a computer and this certainly is the view of the Club of Rome, acknowledged, for example, in an interview by Thiemann (1973b). There is considerable difficulty in specifying the extent to which the constraints posed in the Meadows study actually exist. Even greater uncertainty surrounds most of the other issues which the Club of Rome consider collectively as the world problematique. Because widely differing values influence the perception of risks in trading off long-term against short-term hazards and global against local problems, opinions about the seriousness of any given situation are bound to differ. In such an atmosphere of uncertainty, the use of an apparently rigorous mathematical treatment has undoubted advantage as an effective tool for propaganda.

Many people have taken the position that, whatever its failings, at least it has drawn attention to the issues. Without agreeing that this posture is justified, Lord Ashby (1973), for example, concludes that it is likely that, without the dramatic presentation, public interest would not have been aroused. This may well be true: to take an example, Freeman (1971) notes that there was a decided lack of interest in a previous (completely unconnected and non-computerized) MIT report on critical environmental problems. Even so, in 'The computer that printed out WOLF', Carl Kaysen (1972) points out an obvious danger in exaggerating or overselling computer results. In the Sussex Critique (Cole and coworkers, 1973), the Science Policy Research Unit deliberately used computer output to emphasize criticisms of the MIT Models which others had argued without a computer but also without success.

A member of the Club of Rome has answered criticisms as follows: 'Admittedly, it ["The limits to growth" study] is a faltering and imperfect beginning, but the most contemptible critics are those which denounce it for not having explored the whole of this vast new field and for not having given all the answers' (King, 1974). Our view is that searching and detailed criticism is an integral part of scientific endeavour. One may applaud the MIT modellers for the idea of building a model while depreciating errors, inconsistencies and naive assumptions. There are obvious dangers in the suggestion that 'any model is better than no model'.

By gaining publicity partially through the use of exotic methods, the Club has made contact with high-level decision makers and politicians, as evidenced by the recent meeting in Strasbourg and Hanover, in accordance with Tanter's prescription of seeking out like-minded politicians. However, even if this success is not a 'one off' phenomenon as Kaysen indicates, in the long run the tactic may simply have a muted effect or worse, and in this there is a real danger which may rebound on the scientific community at large, undermining their credibility in future 'crisis' situations.

However carefully an analysis is carried out, once the results have been presented, they are largely out of the researchers' hands. Therefore the manner of presentation is of special importance. Further, the reactions to *The Limits to Growth* and to the Sussex Critique were not based solely on their written content. Rather, public reaction was a response to the reinterpretation by press and other mass media which held certain beliefs about the commitments of the various authors. There is more overlap between the two books than is normally acknowledged. Conversely, although the message of the Club of Rome 'Commentary' (published in *The Limits to Growth*) is quite different from the content of *The Limits to Growth* itself, and very different from the prescription in *World Dynamics*, they have tended to be tarred with the same brush. If the intended message of the Club of Rome was lost or misrepresented, as claimed by Peccei (1973b), it is unfortunate. But reaction to the earlier *World Dynamics* model should have been enough to warn that attention would focus on the computer output. Most of the major criticisms of the model were in fact discussed to some degree in the 'Commentary'. Despite the 'extreme urgency' expressed there in getting the message of World 3 across, simple tests such as those described in the Sussex Critique, which need have delayed publication only slightly, might have avoided a lot of unwelcome criticism. It has always been commonplace for subtleties, such as that the MIT Report was *to* rather than *of* the Club of Rome, to get lost in the headlines.

In setting up the Department of the Environment modelling group, the UK government were clearly wary of such dangers and recognized the need for independent research groups outside government to be concerned with longer-term issues. Tinker (1972), reporting the setting up of the Systems Analysis Unit, suggests the reasons for the government's view:

There are several reasons why this should be so, but the main one is political. The conclusions of Meadows's MIT team are regarded in Whitehall as both unpalatable and unreliable. The idea of an official unit of government coming out with similar reports is not attractive. Let the work be done as far away from the corridors of power as possible. Let it be published freely and be subjected to detailed scientific criticism. Let the non-scientific press retail its conclusions to the public, so that it becomes clear whether or not popular opinion is prepared to accept the measures necessary to reverse undesirable trends. After a few years of scientific and public discussion, most of the nasty ideas will have gone away, and the politicians will safely be able to implement those which are found to be both necessary and expedient.

To the outsider this may seem an unduly cynical approach. To Whitehall it appears the only one which is practical. *The Limits to Growth* may well not be technically sound, and the action it suggests to governments would be impossible in a democratic society unless it had the support of public opinion. Indeed, there is a strong element in the make-up of all politicians which causes them to disbelieve the validity of any analysis until the remedies have become politically palatable. But it is already clear from the public statements of Peter Walker (the then Environment Minister) and a few of his colleagues that they are prepared to take certain risks to help push public opinion maybe in the right direction.

Establishing research of this kind outside government perhaps solves some of the problems of getting a balanced presentation of issues.

Even so, we would argue that the total separation of the scientist and his political person, consciously active or otherwise, is impossible and that there is a difficult personal and collective choice as to how the one may be used to further the other. In futures research, the dilemma is particularly acute. One area of agreement between Sussex and the MIT team (in their debate in *Futures*, March 1973) was that 'the model chosen to describe the real world is an inextricable part of one's values, interests, hopes and fears'. While a scientist's view of the world and the facets of it that he chooses to study reflect legitimately his interests and values, this does not imply that he can no longer study them as a scientist and make his policy suggestions accordingly. There may be no way to resolve such basic disagreements as to 'man's place in the global system' but there are ways of determining with some degree of precision what kinds of methods are likely to pass the critique of other scientists and, what is more, the kinds of policies that are likely to lead to a given result and in what circumstances. A high quality and balance of academic criticism and comment is an even more important safeguard in futures research than in most conventional academic research.

It may be that, even collectively, researchers will be unable to avoid some degree of bias in their work, although it is to be hoped that this can keep within bounds which avoid the creation of public and official scepticism. Futures research and forecasting has many roles, but insofar as one of these is to bring a scientific rigour to bear on the evaluation of long-term policy options, public scepticism ultimately only reduces the value of research. This does not mean that scientists should not be courageous and adventurous. For different reasons the work of scientists such as Galileo, Darwin and Heisenberg had tremendous impact on public thinking. Their theories infringed doctrinal or established patterns of thought, just as did those of Luther, Malthus and Marx. However, there are unhappy precedents of theories being twisted to suit a doctrine and, however unintentional it may be, and however worthy the doctrine, the result may still be harmful.

MODELS AS PART OF THE SOCIAL PROCESS

Unfortunately, the impenetrability of large-scale computer models in fore-casting can easily thwart or disturb public discussion if misused. Furthermore, they may tend to produce an atmosphere of inevitability about the forecast future in the public's, and policy maker's, mind, so there is a possibility of self-fulfilling but unwelcome prophesy. However, it would be wrong to ex-aggerate this aspect without noting that precisely the same effect is produced by over-authoritative sounding proclamations originating from a whole variety of other techniques (some of them purely personal). The main distinc-tion between semantic social theories and a computer model representation of them is that the authenticity conferred by quantification may be more apparent than real. (In fact, what we have been engaged on in this book is largely a 'technology assessment' of the computerization of social models, although inevi-tably our assessment is coloured by the social models to which we subscribe.)

Leaving this comparison aside, it may be argued that, if the description of social structure in any model is accepted and used as a basis for public policy, the model may be reinforced, giving rise to a more rigid societal structure for policy decisions. Whether such a 'feedback' from social theory to social structure is a good or a bad thing depends on circumstances and on one's point of view. It seems likely that, for example, Keynes's prescriptive economic theory has promoted changes of this kind. Similarly the identification of the concept of social class, which, in some ideologies, exists to be destroyed, leads to the collecting of information (through social surveys and the like) about the persistence of class differences; yet this very activity, which is essential to discussion and analysis, reinforces the concept and the 'fact' of those differen-ces. Allen (1973) has argued that academic social scientists perform a 'highly political function' of rationalizing and reinforcing the *status quo* in Britain.

He points out that academic theories eventually permeate society and become the commonsense attitudes of the man in the street. This arises, he says, 'because conventional static theorising tends to certify the existing power relations and to insulate the system from criticism, they are projected throughout society as the only valid explanations. They enter into the ideological process and emerge in an abbreviated, often vulgarised, sloganised form, embedded in language and thought processes alike' (*Times Higher Education Supplement*, February 8, 1974).

SOME SOCIAL IMPLICATIONS

In any case, the chances of reaching a high level of precision in anticipating the long-term future, using models or any other method, are low. All methods attempt to forecast using an inadequate data and theory base drawn from a time span often shorter than the forecasting period. The performance of models should obviously improve as data and theory are mutually improved. However, as explained in the previous chapter, full calibration and verification of complex models is virtually impossible in present circumstances. Consequently a high level of confidence in the results of such computer simulation models is misplaced. Currently, we are probably at the stage where, apart from the point of view of experiment, the advantages of having a global model (i.e. one with no externalities) are outweighed by the additional technical and manipulation problems such models bring. If this is a fair assessment, a number of other conclusions may be drawn with regard to the making of forecasts, policies based upon these forecasts and the way in which policies are implemented.

Our ability to make long-term forecasts of many social phenomena, such as population growth or elasticity of demand for commodities, would be poor even if the physical and technical environment were known exactly. In any case, it might be argued that it is precisely with regard to these considerations that there should be a maximum of public debate. For many policy purposes, current forecasts would be rendered no less reliable if a range of plausible assumptions based upon best expert judgement were made with regard to many social factors. Policies should be designed, as far as possible, to accommodate this range of eventualities. The principle of 'keeping options open' is generally recognized by policy makers, but is often neglected by forecasters in that they tend not to specify the range of policy options available.

The present position is that futures research aimed at deducing guidelines for policy is difficult and full of uncertainties. Similarly, even with the best of intentions, the successful implementation of policies and the achievement of desirable goals by institutions will inevitably be frustrated to some degree by unforeseeable events. To the extent that this situation can be accommodated in public, official and research thinking about the future, there is a chance of striking the right balance of confidence with regard to futures research and the future.

There are few 'ground rules' for matching policy to situations of greater complexity and uncertainty. A fairly high level of diversity within and between the strategies chosen by different policy bodies may in many respects be as effective and as robust to unforeseen changes as uniform coordinated strategies. The kind of policy issues considered by world modellers aim at reconciling short-term and long-term objectives. Since the long-term future is least accessible to definition, an attempt to reduce the time horizon for many policies (i.e. to shorten the period between, for example, an investment decision and its physical realization) may be required, in addition to attempts to extend the period for satisfactory forecasts. Therefore, policies to be *implemented* should probably, as far as is possible, be short-term, but designed within the framework of an 'options open' long-term strategy which is thus subject to regular reassessment.

The search for what is the 'right' treatment of social variables in world models remains inconclusive. As we will consider later, even the *potential* status of such models as policy tools must remain in doubt. The posture of System Dynamics is that a formal model is necessarily better since all the assumptions are displayed and therefore better for aiding policy decisions; but the real mechanism by which policies are formed is inestimably more complicated than even the most complex of computer models, since it is essentially the collective model of very many people. Although no-one would argue that *this* model is anywhere near perfect, or suggest that models are entirely without use as guides and as a means of communication for individuals or policy making bodies, it does provide a yardstick against which the ultimate value of models, however holistic and 'proven' they may be, can be judged.

There is evidence to show that people are far more likely to accept the results of policies they have had a hand in formulating. Given the inevitable uncertainty of achieving a desired future, it could be argued that wider public responsibility is an important component of policy making for the long-term future. One body of literature emphasizes the importance of individual representation in the process of public and private policy making, and particularly in decisions concerning organization of their life styles. For example, Blauner (1960) shows that job satisfaction depends on personal control of the use of one's time and physical movement, and of one's social and technical environment. In general, the greater the degree of control, the greater is the job satisfaction.

As well as the positive aspects of participation, many authors have indicated the negative aspects of restriction. Brehm (1970) makes the point that, in situations where people are restrained from expressing their views, they often react beyond their normal inclination in the direction opposed to those policies which institutions are attempting to impose. Full discussion of this topic, again, goes far beyond the scope of the present book, but is one of the prime considerations relevant to attitudes regarding the future use of models in policy.

Because futures research is on the whole no less exclusive than any other, there is indeed a need to open up the discussion to wider audiences through various media; to have succeeded in this is perhaps the main achievement of *The Limits to Growth*. But to the extent that the use of computers and other sophisticated methods can serve to exaggerate the validity of projections, and thus create a sense of fatality, they erect a barrier between the public, which feels unqualified to quarrel with a computer, and discussion of the future. This is a pity since, outside science fiction, rather little effort is made in speculation about the future to relate prognoses to the life style of individuals. Forecasting 'techniques' are, of course, essential to help researchers but their communication with a wider audience would be improved if they did not rely quite so much on the magic of methods whose potential and limitations can only be appraised by experts. The legitimacy of the experiment to impress the public with the 'accuracy' of the computer must therefore remain open to question, even within the advocacy process of government.

CHANNELS OF COMMUNICATION

At this stage, it is necessary to relate the last considerations to the earlier discussion in Chapter 3 of the role of models in forecasting. As indicated there, where one formally starts in the process of forecasting depends on the general approach and, particularly on whether it is nominated as 'deterministic' or 'normative' and on whether one is primarily concerned with demonstrating 'desirable', 'possible' or 'probable' futures.

The particular approach adopted may be cultural; for example, the French National Plan is firmly based on a scenario or 'prospective' approach while in the United States the work of the Hudson Institute and the MIT modellers has a stronger deterministic element. However, national or cultural factors cannot easily be separated as being the reason for employing a particular method in a given environment, and probably just as important are the personal predispositions of the researchers, including their disciplinary training and expertise.

It is clear that of the three forecasting 'activities' identified in Chapter 3, creating images of the future, especially utopian visions, is the most demanding of imagination and is the most highly 'value laden' part of planning and forecasting exercises, and consequently likely to be the least amenable to rigorous analysis. Arriving at planning decisions and policies too is highly demanding of intuition and opportunism in recognizing the viability of compromises between competing objectives and constraints. The stages of projection, visualization and planning are intertwined and the formation of policy suggestions and policies is a highly iterative and experimental process involving many modifications. Furthermore, this exercise forms part of the activity of many interrelated institutions, academic, public, and governmental, which form the political process in the widest sense. Hence, any one forecasting exercise is part of an evolving process.

Consequently, to be successful, a forecasting exercise must communicate, to a greater or lesser degree, with three bodies of opinion. These are, first, the 'peer group' of academic researchers and professionals; secondly, the decision makers, politicians and planners who will make suggestions for policy which can be tested by a model or will balance suggestions made by researchers against other competing political forces; and thirdly, there is the public at large. Again, with a considerable degree of oversimplification, it may be seen that the most common interface of these three bodies of opinion is likely to be with the projection, decision and scenario components of a forecasting exercise respectively.

In the main, only professional researchers will be able to judge the validity of a particular model and be familiar with its detailed workings, data and assumptions. Politicians and government officials will, of course, be concerned with the reliability of projections, but their faith is more usually indirect through their confidence in individual researchers and consultants and through their proven 'track record'. They will also be concerned with the 'prospective', the vision of the future, but again often in a fairly indirect way through its public interpretation by various media and the electorate. To a fair degree, their concern must be with the production of 'acceptable' policies and in this sense their interest will centre on compromises suggested by the research. For similar reasons, the 'public at large' are likely to interact most successfully with the 'prospective' since this is the most easily presented in a literary and visual way, with a high degree of interpretation superimposed on the broad trends explored by the projections. The network of communication represented by this description is indicated in Figure 9.

Clearly, if this picture corresponds at all to reality, a great deal of trust between scholars and the public and government (and vice versa) is needed.

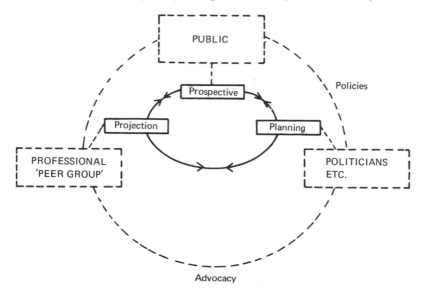

Figure 9. Communication from forecasting activities to societal groups

Academics particularly, since they at least should appreciate the difficulties of reaching correct assessments on most of the issues considered as 'world problems', have an obligation to be careful to develop the appropriate channels and modes of presentation.

In Chapter 5, a 'flow diagram' (Figure 8) illustrating the iterative stages involved in the construction and testing of large-scale computer models was presented.

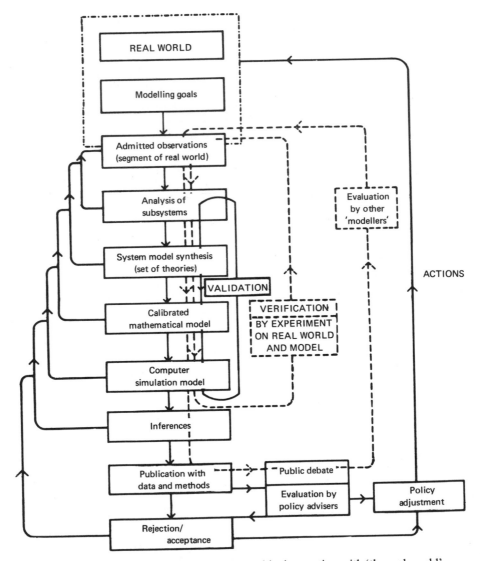

Figure 10. The model building process and its interaction with 'the real world'

The iterative nature of the modelling process was emphasized particularly with regard to testing via validation and verification. But the creation of theories incorporated in a model is a collective activity. This activity is largely focused on the 'peer group' of professional researchers and others concerned with a particular theoretical issue. However, the interaction of theories with society at large (the real world) via publication, politicians and so on, must also be taken into account in a more complete representation of the modelling process.

Thus, Figure 8 is revised to include the evaluation of other modellers (and indeed others in the same research group). Communication and publication of large modelling projects creates particular problems. Because of the difficulty of gaining a level of consensus in complex policy issues, where virtually all currently used theories are inadequate and precise data unavailable, we have suggested that models are rarely likely to be accepted as 'objective' and adopted totally by all parties to a decision. Any model is therefore best viewed as a component part of the advocacy process. (Incidentally this is the position often taken by Forrester, that the role of a model is to help people subscribing to a particular view to evaluate it more rigorously. We have little quarrel with this. Our chief concern and contention with this approach is the status of the underlying assumptions, and the suggestion implicit in Forrester's writings that the mere act of quantification automatically confers authenticity upon policy recommendations.)

Finally, we have mentioned earlier the inseparable nature of theories about society and society itself. Theories, directly or indirectly, via policies at all levels, or technological or cultural innovations, help to determine the shape of society. Because social theories, unlike physical theories, are so often prescriptive, it seems reasonable to consider that society seeks to be a reflection of idealised models of social systems, just as theories aim to represent those systems. Thus in completing our representation of the modelling process (Figure 10), we indicate this aspect of the model as an inseparable part of the social process.

7

Assessment and Challenge for the Future

Previous chapters have described some of the forces which have led to the recognition of the need for a planning and forecasting device such as a world model and the belief that building a useful model is a reasonable objective at the present time for many so-called world problems. To evaluate this idea, we have considered in turn (a) how the current level of theoretical knowledge in several disciplines can contribute to a comprehensive global model, (b) the manner in which the correct organization of scientific endeavour and inter-disciplinary research is essential to the success of this kind of model building activity, (c) the state-of-the-art in terms of the techniques for building and (especially) for testing models, in relation to a conceptual model of the modelling process, and (d) the extent and success of models in application in terms of forecasting ability, as aids to policy formation and the publicizing of particular points of view.

Although the dangers in extrapolating from these findings to the case of world models are appreciated, it is both interesting and instructive for us now to consider what interpretations and conclusions may be inferred from these findings for global models, with particular reference to those we have selected for special study. These are the model of Pestel and Mesarovic, the Bariloche Latin American model, the Japanese Club of Rome study and the work of the UK Department of the Environment.

From the description of the second generation of world models in Chapter 2, it may be seen that the purposes for which the new world models are being built vary to some degree. Even though researchers from all of the projects we have described accept that what they are doing is of an experimental and preliminary nature, they are nevertheless understandably eager to influence public policy. We would therefore, in part, wish to approach an assessment of the models from the point of view of their being relevant to policy. Modellers, in any case, stress the urgency of the world problems their research is concerned with, so that, even if the work is exploratory, its time scale for convincing results should not be too extended. However, we also recognize the possible catalytic role of models as a behavioural device for stimulating and structuring debate and for indicating gaps and shortcomings in theory and facilitating interdisciplinary communication.

Before making the following remarks about on-going modelling projects, we emphasize the immense difficulties which, to a greater or lesser degree, researchers are endeavouring to overcome in what, at the very least, must be considered as valuable pioneering efforts. Thus, if our remarks about specific aspects of projects or techniques appear over critical in terms of a full recognition of the technical and other problems to be overcome, it is in the spirit of practising modellers who are also indulging in a great deal of self-questioning. This is especially true of remarks concerned with the original world models of Forrester and Meadows, which have sometimes provided convenient examples for discussion simply because of our own audience's familiarity with these works.

From the presentation of the Mesarovic–Pestel model at IIASA in 1974, it was possible to obtain a reasonably full picture of the development of the work about two years after the beginning of the project, and just prior to the publication of their popular book. Much of the earlier work had been taken up with data collection and the testing of exploratory ideas. Thus perhaps six months only had been spent in actually programming the various sub-models. A great deal of valuable effort had been put into assembling useful comprehensive time-series data which appears to be fairly consistently matched across the regions considered. It can be argued that data of this kind would not have been coordinated except in the context of such a modelling effort. A further technical contribution of the work lies in details of particular sub-system models. Whatever value the model itself may ultimately have, this work may well prove a valuable contribution towards the further understanding and resolution of world problems. Several potential technical problems were evident which would also not be easy to resolve; for example, there is the problem of linking together quite complex sub-models of very different levels of aggregation. It might, therefore, be considered that much of the apparently highly detailed description in some of the sub-models is superfluous to the model (as a comprehensive global model) unless other subsystems are brought up to a corresponding level of detail. (Nevertheless, this detail may be more relevant to sensible discussion of particular issues.) Also, the question of model testing had not been satisfactorily resolved, although we would consider that, as yet, adequate methods do not exist even if the necessary data are available. It may be that the only way round this is to build less ambitious models.

In our view, much uncertainty must remain with regard to the possibility of mapping the hierarchical structure of Mesarovic convincingly into the 'world system' in a manner compatible with the wide range of interests that the model purports to represent. The model is an attempt at an enormous leap in terms of the application of hierarchical control methods over their traditional applications. The rather unsatisfactory experiences of 'gaming' models in conflict theory suggest that much caution should be given to treating such applications as anything other than experiments at this time. The inherent interest and even initial excitement in man–machine exercises should not be misconstrued.

Although we consider that experiment in this direction is of great interest and should be encouraged, we are sceptical about the real value of satellite-linked gaming models. Remote conferencing has yet to be proved to be of real value for even relatively straightforward commercial purposes. From our earlier analysis, we would argue that the chances of producing such a world planning tool for use immediately (or even in the next decade) must be remote in the absence of corresponding political institutions. One can only rephrase an earlier question and ask where the world regional planners with any authority and responsibility to represent 'Europe' or 'South Asia' are, and who will consent to sit at a satellite-linked computer terminal? Nevertheless, we believe that, with a more modest objective in a better defined problem area, a real contribution might eventually be made by such an arrangement.

This point was brought out clearly at a demonstration of the Mesarovic–Pestel model to six members of the European Parliament in Hanover in February 1975. While the Parliamentarians generally felt that the exercise had been useful and that models could be used as an input into the policy-making process, they stressed the diverse nature of this process, with factors such as pressure groups and mass media exerting a certain amount of influence in decision making. The value of models was considered to be more indirect, i.e. as useful bases for discussion and for drawing up conceptual guidelines for policy. The Parliamentarians also pointed out the need for modellers to inspire confidence in the validity of their work before results could be considered seriously, a point we have emphasized earlier.

As considered earlier, continuity of funding is likely to present problems for long-term projects of this scale, and this may explain the prevalence of somewhat premature publication. We are aware of suggestions to develop the model further in one or other of the international research institutes. Although the size of the model makes it difficult for commentators to obtain full details of all aspects through conventional publication, we would consider that work in outside organizations is possible, provided that project members transfer with the model. Even with this, one might suspect that (just as happened with the attempted reapplications of the Meadows model) the model would undergo rapid and extensive changes or even the setting up of an entirely new model structure.

Our concern in respect of the Mesarovic–Pestel model is that it may be seen as a *general* planning tool, and certainly it was presented as such at its uncovering at IIASA. Equally, in view of the fact that the model was at that time quite obviously in a preliminary stage of development, the firmness of the conclusions conveyed in *Mankind at the Turning Point* and of the presentation in Washington strike one as surprising (e.g. Mesarovic and Pestel, 1974a, p. 157).

The Mesarovic–Pestel Model is the only 'general purpose' world model designed to convey the Club of Rome's message to the governments of all nations. Like World 3, it will inevitably be criticized as portraying a peculiarly western view of the world. From the presentation in Washington, it is apparent that the use of the model to the Club of Rome is similar to that of the MIT models. The 'advertisement' value of big models has been commented on earlier and, insofar as the findings of the model confirm the predilections of the Club, they will be used as 'evidence'. This remark should not be taken as entirely critical: it is almost inevitable that, given the current state of theory, results will tend to confirm foregone conclusions; and we believe that in this situation it is to the advocacy role that such 'viewpoint' models are most suited.

In comparison with the Mesarovic–Pestel model, the Latin American project has rather limited ambitions and a more compact structure. The researchers in charge of the project have a similar political outlook and overtly acknowledge that the purpose of their modelling effort is to demonstrate the logic and relevance of these views. Although the project has Club of Rome support, some members consider the work to be 'utopian' (Peccei, 1973a, 1973b); whether it is less so than the ideal espoused in either of the other Club of Rome projects is a matter for debate and, ultimately, probably a matter of opinion. Within Latin America, the work, if cleverly presented, may also be an effective propaganda instrument. Direct links exist with government (and ex-government) officials in the Argentine, and use is made of characteristically close ties between the academic world and government. As with the Mesarovic–Pestel model, wider publicity is expected to be gained through a popular 'Limits to growth' type of publication. It might be supposed that, although this should have a fair impact in Latin America, it is less likely to be effective outside those countries (except among world modellers).

One important consequence of this work is that a group of researchers, with the capability and confidence to assess work of this kind coming from other groups, now exists in a developing country. One comment worth making here is that much of the work has been carried out on a small (16K GEC Bull) computer, which is in some contrast to the size of machine often considered 'essential' to the building of such large models. It seems likely that, because of its relatively modest objectives and competent team work, the project will be completed satisfactorily and published by the end of 1975 (about one year behind schedule). Whether this first version of the model will be improved upon is not certain. A disappointment in the project must be that it did not, for a variety of reasons, continue to be a 'Latin American project' involving several nations, as originally envisaged.

In any case, the project has attracted a small team of experienced researchers and well placed 'consultants' and it is one of the few world modelling projects which does *not* have a systems analyst or control engineer as team leader.

Technically and conceptually the project seems to be well conceived in many respects, although we would consider that it shares many of the more fundamental problems we have detailed for other projects. A considerable amount of attention has been paid to the form and calibration of relationships in the model. For example, the demographic sector, which is claimed to be an advance over previous theories, gives a good explanation of life expectancy in terms of socio-economic variables. Even so, 'explanation' does not equal forecasting ability and population projections have been notoriously inconsistent. Further, the sub-model is calibrated on cross-sectional data and this always requires the massive assumption of the equivalence of cross-section and historical data if the model is to be employed for time-series extrapolations.

One novel feature of the Bariloche model is the optimizing routine (one version of which attempts to maximize life expectancy in developing countries as rapidly as possible, given other constraints defined in the model). It is to be questioned whether, given the quality of information that currently has to be used in models, it is better to use a sophisticated optimising algorithm (however technically beautiful it may be) rather than a 'by hand' method, in which researchers experiment intuitively and systematically with the model 'policy' variables. Any 'optimization' routine provides only sub-optimization (except in relatively simple cases) in the sense that it operates with only a limited number of variables in relation to the total set incorporated in the 'mental' model. Nevertheless, guidance and, sometimes, unexpectedly beneficial solutions may be derived by the use of this approach.

In different ways, both the above exercises have attempted to produce models which are less deterministic than *The Limits to Growth;* and it is interesting to compare the approaches. At first sight, the Mesarovic–Pestel model is the least constrained since it employs the hierarchical structure and nominates all variables considered to be difficult to quantify as eligible for the 'norm stratum'. But, as pointed out previously, at our present level of knowledge nearly all parameters in the 'causal stratum'—the deterministic component of the model—must be *selected* and the process of selection itself is a value judgement. In taking a magnitude for, say, the lifetime of a mineral resource or the threshold heat capacity to cause unwanted changes in the biosphere, one is clearly not in the same situation as a chemist using a number for the molecular weight of a compound. (This is not, of course, to pretend that 'choice' does not play an important part in many areas of the 'hard' sciences.) Thus, while at first sight it may seem that the goals to be explored with the Mesarovic–Pestel model have been left open to depend on the wishes of the user, it would be possible to choose objectives which many people might consider reasonable but which simply are not compatible with some of the fundamental assumptions of the deterministic part of the 'Strategy for survival' model. This is because the structure of the causal stratum inevitably sets constraints on choices which may not be agreed upon. It may be that using the 'hierarchical' structure makes this less inevitable than, for example, in *The Limits to Growth* model and also makes the identification of such areas of disagreement easier. The goal of a stable equilibrium society used in that model was one stemming from the philosophies of the environmental movement; this was a utopian goal and an end in itself, as much as the consequence of a belief in the urgency imposed by finite physical limits to certain 'growth' processes. However, because of the assumption of narrow physical limits, it was not possible to change the goal of the model to one of a growth equilibrium (i.e. a dynamically balanced supply and demand taking account of social and technological changes) without simultaneously adopting a different description of what constitutes a 'physical' resource.

Again, in constrast to the Mesarovic–Pestel model, the Bariloche model explicitly takes normative views. However, given its starting point, which is a particular socio-economic configuration, and the objective function of the model, which is a certain 'economic' goal to be achieved in as short a time as possible, the model operates in a highly deterministic manner. Since the Bariloche team believe that the prevailing socio-economic structure of developing countries, specifically Latin American countries, makes rapid equitable development impossible, the team does not attempt to model the current situation. They model instead the situation which would prevail if a certain political and economic reorientation were to come about. Thus the aftermath of *this* change is the starting point for the model runs. From this point, however, birth rate, life expectancy and similar parameters are rigidly calculated from the allocation of resources (through the optimizing routine of the model). Hence, although the causal life expectancy model gives a good regression fit of life expectancy and fertility against nutrition, education etc., the possibilities of specific actions such as birth-control propaganda campaigns or legislation, whose potential effectiveness may well be considered a matter of judgement, are not explicitly accounted for as they might be in the Mesarovic–Pestel model.

The Japanese Club of Rome team have adopted what is perhaps the most innovative approach to modelling, experimenting with several formulations and patterns of assumptions. The attempt to provide a continuous description of the world distribution of wealth, for example, has shown up some of the difficulties of achieving a description which treats the world realistically as an evolving system rather than as a collection of rigidly defined interacting regions. Similarly, the attempt to bring together long-term and short-term interactions has pointed to some of the issues which determine the forces stabilizing economic growth. The project has concentrated largely on Japanese national interests in relation to the world at large, thus attempting to reinforce the importance of global issues in the mind of decision makers within existing national political institutions. It has a wide forum for expositions of its findings through the Club of Rome, through the Japanese academic environment (the project is located at the elite Kyoto University and has the support of the Japanese Techno-economic Society) and in government circles (through its sponsors, the Japanese Ministry of International Trade and Industry).

Of all the world modelling projects considered by us, the project of the Systems Analysis Research Unit in the UK Department of Environment has perhaps the closest permanent link with high-level government officials. The DOE probably provides the best access to advocates in government who believe both in the importance of *The Limits to Growth* issues and the potential value of systems analytic studies.

Location within government provides some advantages for modellers wishing to influence government, and for gaining access to information (such as resource endowments) which might otherwise be considered strategic or confidential. On the other hand, civil servants are typically constrained in their freedom to publicize their results. There is, in addition, often a traditional reticence to expose government research to outside comment. Our view, as stressed elsewhere in this book, is that, especially when research is of a tentative or 'experimental' nature, it is important that results are exposed to a wider audience than government in-house research normally receives. This helps to ensure not only that results and conclusions receive the fullest academic evaluation, but also that, in the case of more speculative research about global and social futures, a high level of public awareness and discussion is achieved.

In fact, for a number of reasons, including those mentioned above, it seems that full discussion of in-house government work in this area has not been achieved despite a number of presentations at 'invited audience' seminars. To open up work fully to outside criticism (particularly in the UK structure) is difficult and, so far, what has occurred is that 'assumptions' are fairly well discussed but data are not. Unfortunately, the two cannot be entirely divorced. As explained earlier in setting up the project, the somewhat sceptical UK Government was acutely aware of the possible repercussions of governments carrying out and publishing controversial studies. This situation is in some contrast to the work in the US Environmental Protection Agency, which has thus far been given more extensive exposure (see, for example, House (1973)).

As explained in Chapter 2, the Department of the Environment work relies, to some degree, on other modelling projects and is of a rather similar structure. The work has also been innovative, in, for example, attempting to set up an energy input/output accounting framework for various sectors in the model. The main functions of this work put forward by the researchers is to demonstrate the importance in the UK context of planning ahead, particularly in relation to carrying out research and development into new technologies as an insurance for the future and trying to spot 'blockages' in the technological system.

Consequently, provided that the programme of research is not too susceptible to changes in government policy (and this is likely to depend on the support of individuals in government sympathetic to the approach), it would appear that the group will be able to make some contribution. However, if there are no groups outside government having a similar role to the National Institute of Economic and Social Research and the London Business School with respect to the Treasury models, and if there is not a better public forum, the much needed professional and lay criticism will be lacking.

INPUTS TO MODELLING AND REQUIREMENTS FOR THEIR EXPLOITATION

Will world models prove to be a passing fashion, or will they become more widely accepted and used in the future? In our opinion they can provide a powerful means of representing certain ideas and theories—a critical question is whether these inputs are, or can be made, sufficiently firm and rigorous to permit quantitative treatment.

Common to all models is the problem that current theoretical understanding of a whole range of social, ecological and other processes is limited, and to an unknowable extent. Furthermore, there is no guarantee that sufficiently rapid and balanced progress in understanding the problems considered by global modellers will be made. Although we expect steady advances to be achieved in understanding ecological systems, for example, the same may not be true for many social systems.

In the social sciences, it may be that understanding will always lag behind the immediate needs of practical policy issues. While the physical sciences can be viewed as a sequence of paradigm changes, these are accepted because additional phenomena have come to light and the new world view does represent 'progress' in the sense that these additional phenomena can be explained. For example, despite the advent of quantum mechanics, Newton's laws still hold good within their domain of validity. In the social sciences, however, the 'rules' according to which economies and societies run appear to change, because of changes in mankind's situation and his increase in knowledge about that situation. This means that a change of paradigm may be necessary not merely because some new, previously unexperienced, process cannot be explained under the old structure, but because the latter has begun to fail to account for phenomena it previously described adequately. A contemporary example may be that of Keynes's General Theory, which suggests that unemployment is due to insufficient demand which cannot coexist with inflation; in the 1930s and for some time thereafter this idea appeared to be correct, but recent experience appears to show it to be inadequate. The current inability of macroeconomic theory to explain many national and international phenomena suggests, if anything, a general regression in performance, as reflected in the apparent worsening of many economic forecasts. In general, models are not good at forecasting in turbulent conditions or (even in the physical sciences) able to forecast well discontinuities or other critical phenomena.

Despite the overall lack of a permanent and solid theoretical foundation, there is certainly a need for modelling projects to be keyed into the best theory which is currently available. One serious criticism of the MIT modellers was that, despite their working in a department containing some of the world's best-known economists, the models were constructed with scarcely any reference to the considerable relevant literature available. We take the position that it is the theory rather than the computer model which is important to the understanding of issues, and that it is the solution to the world's problems rather than the solutions to the problems of modelling which are sought, although we would not have written our book if we thought that the solution to the latter problems would not contribute to the former. This means, however, that modellers must have direct access to theory within the research group, which must, therefore, be strongly interdisciplinary and not, as so often happens, largely composed of 'modellers'.

An interdisciplinary research group will possess a diffuse model distributed among the team members. The members of such research groups are usually chosen or self-chosen to be compatible, so that, even if they do not have precisely the same views, they are at least able to work together and communicate, and thus reach a common perspective. The consensus view of the research group will be its 'paradigm' and will be reflected in its collective model. The extent to which any particular group employs modelling methods to structure internal debate and facilitate communication with outsiders depends very much on the particular expertise and style of the group members. For this to be achieved, a threshold competence in understanding of the technical and other principles involved is essential. Given this, we believe that by attempting to 'interface' different aspects of the same problem, or common aspects of different problems, through the use of a mathematical or structured analysis, new theoretical insights are likely to emerge and individual researchers will extend their expertise and overall understanding. However, we are sceptical whether this experience can really be readily conveyed to casual users, as, for example, in some kinds of gaming exercise involving decision makers which have been suggested.

MANIPULATION OF INPUTS—SCALE AND METHODS OF REPRESENTATION

It is certain that much of our inability to explain social processes arises because they really are exceedingly complex. But it is also certain that many apparently complex macro-processes result from the superimposed behaviour of many similar micro-processes (such as the behaviour of individuals or, in the case of world models, individual nations!). Although these small-scale processes are often intuitively apparent and thus are, at least in part, empirically recognizable, they often cannot be isolated and examined or experimented with independently. The only way to examine these rigorously often seems to be through a fairly complex model (often involving the use of a computer).

There are many 'local' problems which cannot be reasonably isolated from the wider context. It is obviously very difficult to decide when exogenous factors are so important as to require their being internalized as subsystems in a model. As explained in Chapter 6, although, until recently, foreign demand etc. have usually been estimated externally to economic forecasting models, a realization of the need to 'endogenize' is growing. At what point does this need become apparent? Certainly, when exogenous factors contribute a significant amount (in planning or theoretical terms) to the behaviour of internal factors and are also themselves significantly affected by internal factors. A model of the Japanese economy, for example, must take account of world events; but must a model of world events take account, specifically, of what happens in Japan? Clearly, the answer must be that it depends on the precise details of the information that are required.

Inevitably, the quality of available inputs for some processes will be particularly weak. Even if considered to be relevant to the problem in hand, care should be taken that such issues are not so poorly understood or difficult to quantify that error introduced by their inclusion does not outweigh inaccuracies caused by their exclusion. Pollution is an example; it constituted the least well researched sector of World 3, but was important to the behaviour of the model and also was vital to the attention attracted to the model. While it can be argued that pollution could become a major factor limiting industrial growth, the available data, such as it is, allows for other interpretations which many people would argue are more reasonable. In particular, as pointed out by Marstrand and Sinclair (1973), it seems that the main threats in pollution are not global but local and could be dealt with by political and technological developments discounted by the MIT researchers.

This is, nevertheless, not to say that a model which demonstrates how specific pollutants are transported around the globe would not be extremely valuable and worth striving for. Such a model highlights issues of international conse-quence such as the likely amounts of pollution generated in one country crossing the frontiers of others. In many situations models dealing with specific global issues, i.e. individual world subsystem models, may often be, on balance, more appropriate than world models. There is the advantage that theories and data referring to a specific issue are usually more compatible than those used in coupled subsystems, and that one can choose to model on the computer only those issues, or the particular facets of them considered to be amenable to the technique. For example, a global pollution transport model would be based on established physical and chemical principles and formulae (although neither the precise manner in which these factors should be accounted for nor the necessary data are yet known, nor is the full range of algorithms needed to carry out the computation). The difficulty, of course, is that even particularly simple world problems such as this tend to be 'hybrids' concerning several academic disciplines, so one cannot in practice designate any world problem as purely 'physical'. Some are, of course, more 'physical' than others and one would expect environmental and shortage problems to be easier to study through computer modelling than many social problems. On a lower level still, quantitative techniques can be used only to examine very specific questions within a subsystem. Using linear programming to solve well-defined distribution problems gives an example of rather precise application of the computer; for example, on the basis of assumptions about costs of transportation and storage etc., it may be possible to find a range of low cost solutions to the problem of citing international granaries, one of which might be acceptable even after less tangible (e.g. political) factors are considered.

In some ways, then, computer methods can be expected to be more valuable when applied in a more restricted way. We strongly agree with Forrester and Meadows, however, that the less tangible aspects of a problem should not be ignored and we are certainly not suggesting this. The question of whether or not they should be included in a computer model, which then gives a 'complete' representation of the issue at hand, or whether they should be treated by other methods, depends on the purpose of the analysis. We consider that, in most cases, the best method of directly attacking a problem is to use an eclectic approach: all available methods should be considered and computer modelling should be employed where it is thought to be the most valuable technique. This approach helps to avoid the particular danger that all aspects of the problem will be forced into a 'physical' mould; in their determination to quantify, some modellers have tended to underrate or be insensitive to the importance of highly relevant social and political processes. Nevertheless, it should be recognized that many of the deficiencies of computer models are implicit in any other method, formal or intuitive, and the compromise with regard to technique required to achieve the best forecasting performance must be made carefully. We would stress the value of large computer models for the less direct benefits we have already discussed: as indicating possible interconnections between phenomena, as a means of articulating viewpoints and theories, as highlighting points of weakness in available theory and data, and in facilitating communication.

In Chapter 3 we spoke of three related activities in forecasting and indicated that the major role of model building activities was in the 'prediction' phase of forecasting (i.e. showing the logical connection between some postulated future and the present). However, from what we have said in the last chapter, it is clear that, in most areas, knowledge is insufficient to permit this connection to be made with any degree of confidence. In fact, we have to recognize that in many areas our ability to predict unambiguously the consequences of events and policies goes little beyond that obtained from a considered extrapolation. Computer models push this extrapolation to its limits, but ultimately the time horizon for satisfactory prediction is constrained by the 'natural' time-scale characteristic of the physical, economic and social processes with which one is concerned.

The longer the time span considered the greater the commitment to a subjective description of the future which subsumes assumptions about these time scales. Thus, as with the models we have described, one is ultimately, explicitly or implicitly, working within a 'scenario' which represents, for example, some assumed or desired long-term strategy. Viewed simply from the requirement to increase the time span of useful predictive forecasts, the value of long-term strategic planning at all levels seems very clear. Given a broadly defined long-term strategy, the usefulness of models to examine shorter-term incremental choices is enhanced.

MUST MODELS BE COMPLEX?

Assuming that the decision to use a large-scale computer model to study, for example, a particular world problem has been taken, we suggest that a primary requirement for the model to be of value is that it should be as *simple* as possible. The purpose of modelling is to simplify to an appropriate level, in order to make things comprehensible and to permit generalizations. In view of the problems of construction, testing and communication, Ockham's razor should be used ruthlessly, no material being included simply 'for the sake of it' as often seems to occur with simulation modelling. This tends to be a self-reinforcing process since the larger a model becomes, the simpler is the relative task of including additional sectors.

It is usually possible to simplify a complex model after construction in such a way that its essential content is retained, as evidenced by a minimal change in its output characteristics. It was pointed out in Chapter 5 that dynamic systems, in particular, are usually at any given time of their evolution dominated by a few of their parameters. It often appears that simplification of a system model to reflect this dominance still leads to a model good enough for its intended application, although it opens the door to the unwarranted application of inferences in other domains and so should be used with care. In general, in a simulation model, simplification is only justified after examining a model which is more complex; it is partly for this reason we have stressed the importance of aggregation, sensitivity and linearization.

Sensitivity testing should be carried out to indicate that all variables included have an influence on output such that, if any variables were omitted, different inferences would be possible over the domain of application of the model. Within its preassigned structure, the model would then be 'reduced' to the simplest possible form. Sensitivity testing is also a crucial method of checking 'robustness'; it should be carried out to the extent that the modeller can satisfy himself, and his peer group, that the main inferences he draws from his model are not affected by any combination of values given to the variables used within their recognized limits of error.

If linearization of a complex model is feasible to any extent in a model which incorporates social elements and which provides a reasonably accurate representation of reality, the implication is that complex interations at a 'micro' level are sufficiently 'random' in nature to permit the use of simple statistical laws at the 'macro' level. As discussed previously, this situation frequently occurs in the natural sciences and is an important reason for the 'success' of these disciplines. It therefore would be of great value to obtain more information on the circumstances under which linearization or the 'law of large systems' are valid; it would then be possible to choose the 'simplest' representation of a particular system in advance. Satisfactory statistical methods for the simultaneous validation of models as complex as global models with several hundred or even thousands of equations have yet to be devised, although some progress has been made in this direction in various fields.

Several statistical techniques for multivariate analysis are available to extract those parameters which lead to a concise form for a model while retaining a sufficient level of explanation. A less highly parameterized description of a system is easier to handle and explore satisfactorily; and since operational justification is found in the fact that, statistically, a given set of observations can 'support' a description with fewer factors, the intuitively identifiable 'reality' of the new variables is supported. It often seems that the virtues of simplicity outweigh those of methods which permit a higher level of 'realism' to be attained.

Generally speaking, although the more sophisticated techniques, such as those involving uncertainty, are likely to be more 'realistic', they are more expensive and time consuming and the effort may not be worthwhile without the backing of adequate theory. In this case, an admittedly unrealistic representation is often adopted. For example, if one merely wishes to experiment with modelling a system in the hope of improving understanding of its operation, nothing beyond a wholly deterministic mechanism-describing model may be needed. We believe that, with 'hybrid' world problems, where the quality and quantity of data is mixed, the best approach is a gradual increase in complexity; one begins by constructing a 'core' model, i.e. a model which takes account of the most important determinants for the long-term development of the system and, in particular, concentrates on those issues for which there is the soundest theoretical base. This model can later be used to 'drive' a set of more tentative sub-models representing other important but so far less well researched problem areas. The advantage of this approach is that it permits best use to be made of available theory and at the same time avoids the hazard of introducing too many tentative relationships into the main body of the model (Clark and coworkers, 1973). Also, the experience gained in working with the smaller model is invaluable in the construction of the more detailed version.

Compared with problems of unsatisfactory inputs, steady progress can be expected with regard to the technical problems associated with modelling. In particular, the constraint of limited computer capacity, where it still exists, is likely to become less important. A reason for the construction of simple models we have not discussed is the apparently high cost of large models which, even if they are successful, may make their contribution poor value for money at the present time. However, although computer-based projects traditionally have been expensive, this has often been because of overpricing by their authors and exaggeration of hardware requirements. Further, the greater cost of building a calibrated model is in the collection of data and the bringing together of relevant expertise; and this is essential whatever method is employed. The marginal cost of using models in a broadly based interdisciplinary group is comparatively small. It cannot be overemphasized that complex nonlinear models are extremely intractable analytically and that only a process of exhaustive investigation can fully explore such a model. For this reason alone, the Rand Corporation have recently summed up modelling advice for social systems modelling as 'model simple, think complex', and with this we readily concur.

THE SOCIAL AND INSTITUTIONAL FRAMEWORK

For several other institutional reasons the possibility of building a global 'policy' model with a role similar to, or enlarging upon, those of the national governments does not exist at the present time. Although United Nations agencies with areas of interest equivalent to national government departments have been set up, the real power of such agencies is strictly limited. Most world modelling work reflects the realization that modellers must attempt to make their findings about global issues relevant to national interests. For this reason, most of the models have been constructed to show a national (or regional) interest 'in the world context'. Nevertheless, a number of international agencies have expressed interest in the possibility of using global models, and are already engaged in a fair amount of large-scale modelling activity. Thus, one might expect that, as the role of these agencies is strengthened (as we believe it ultimately will be), the direct policy relevance of global modelling activities will increase.

International firms may be the first to apply global models in aiding policy strategies which are put into action. Their global interests and relatively well defined objectives make large-scale models a potentially useful forecasting device for them.

Because 'general purpose' planning models have turned out to be irrelevant or at least largely ineffective, it must again be questioned whether it is better to have a set of ready-made subsystems models (as in the Mesarovic–Pestel model) or to construct 'custom built' packages for studying particular issues. In practice, it takes at most a few months to program and validate a computer model provided that sufficient data, theory and expertise are available. Since it seems inevitable that 'long-term' forecasters will always be looking at poorly researched issues, the chance of having precisely the right model 'on the shelf' is limited.

A fair amount of flexibility with regard to this seems reasonable since, in practice, 'trust' is placed in the individuals building the model rather than in the model itself, so that precise details are irrelevant in this sense. Thus, the indirect familiarity and faith in particular models by government officials may outweigh the fact that, for example, it contains a certain amount of superfluous detail.

But, by the same token, unless fairly direct personal contact with government departments or international agencies can be maintained, world models are likely to become as irrelevant as the general-purpose urban and regional models. The channels of communication between modeller and government need to be firmly established; and indeed most world modelling efforts have endeavoured to achieve this through direct contact or through propaganda activities.

We have stressed the need for links with both governments and the public. The experiments of Dator and Krauch, using on-line computer models in association with quite elaborate television expert discussion panels and 'phone-in' facilities for the audience, have been mentioned earlier. At the moment, the role of the computer model in this effort seems to be largely to 'heighten' public awareness, and there must be a danger that too much credibility is placed on the model results in comparison with other comment. We would consider that the right formula for the 'trade-off' between integration of many diverse factors in a highly complex world model and the integration of this model into government, and more especially into public thinking, is far from clear. What is needed here is experimentation, and work undertaken in this spirit should be presented as such.

This raises another issue which goes beyond the territory we have chosen to cover in detail in this book. Because of the inherent uncertainty in forecasting, it follows that any adopted policies have a fair chance of going wrong. This cannot be avoided, but one might argue that the effects of uncertainty would be cushioned if there was more open discussion of many far-reaching public policy issues and their possible implications. There is a need for continued experimentation in this direction, which requires (among other things) that modellers make their results as comprehensible as possible to the lay public and avoid the tendency for their methods to lead to 'mystification.'

It may be argued that if different groups engaged in comparable analyses carried out in a rigorous and scientific manner arrive at a wide range of conclusions, then this range represents the real uncertainty in understanding more truly than any 'standard error' derived from sensitivity testing of any single model. In the case of the eight US economic models described in the last chapter, for example, it turned out that the difference between forecast and 'actual' performance was comparable to the range of projections obtained from the different models, and this information is as useful as the forecasts themselves since it shows the range of uncertainty within which policies are likely to operate.

For several reasons, including the critical capacity noted above, we have strongly advocated the value of fostering a number of reasonably independent research groups inside and outside government related via a peer group arrangement.

In the first place, it is evident that the interdisciplinary research essential to the construction of world models is still in an embryonic stage and, consequently, an effective pluralistic peer group arrangement is not sufficiently developed. Because of the intractable problems of achieving a high level of confidence in the results of a long-term forecasting model in particular (as discussed in Chapter 6), a stable environment with continuity of funding may be considered a prerequisite for the building of a useful model. In fact, few models currently have either stable funding or stable environment. Most projects are on a 'one-off' basis—a fixed contract to 'build a model'—when what is really required for the construction of a complex planning model is the opportunity to update this systematically as empirical evidence determines, while recognizing that the real 'pay-off' is likely to be long-term. A few modelling activities, such as the UK Department of the Environment model, have this stability in a limited sense. Even with funding stability, there is still the problem of holding a viable research group together; again this is very difficult to achieve in the present situation, particularly for the larger models, where the problem of maintaining the necessary cohesion in a diverse group over the period needed to complete a final, partially verified 'working model' could prove to be very difficult. In the long run, the only way to ensure continuity is to have a sufficiently large and competent peer group whose abilities are at least to some degree interchangeable.

Such an arrangement essentially requires some degree of government sponsorship and commitment, whether the work is carried out inside or outside government departments. The precision of forecasts and the complex needs of policy makers, however, mean that it is not immediately clear even then that the right kind of pay-off would be obtained. Nevertheless, the fact that several kinds of models looking at 'physical' and some 'social' questions have fairly consistently proved to be better at forecasting than other methods indicates to us that it is worth persevering with their development both as forecasting devices and as inputs to the social process. As a minimum requirement, therefore, models must be able to forecast better than other methods or offer a more acceptable way of achieving consensus.

CONCLUSIONS

The importance of recognizing and specifying objectives for a modelling activity can hardly be overemphasized. It is not possible simply to 'model a system' in some value-free way. We would argue, therefore, that it is not in any strict sense possible to identify a model as 'normative' or 'deterministic'; any model will inevitably be a mixture of both. However, the dividing line between value-laden and objective statements is also a matter of degree, depending on the level of consensus about particular statements or observations. Whether a model is *called* one thing or the other depends largely on what its authors think they are doing.

None of this is to deny the importance of value judgements or of the need to achieve some recognized kind of objectivity. Indeed an implicit goal of this book is to promote the necessity of rigorous and systematic thought about social problems through the use of modelling methods.

Objectivity is in the eye of the beholder (and in this case also in the mind of the modeller) and to pretend that any model of the world can, at our present level of understanding, be separated from the personalities and values of its builders is naive. But we should not be too sanguine and conclude that, since all models are, to some degree, normative, any model will do. It would be foolish to pretend that social processes do not have considerable momentum and inertia or that the constraints on changes of direction are not severe. The argument among modellers between normative and deterministic approaches is largely about whether processes assumed to have a high degree of built-in inertia really do. For example, the apparent inertia may be a result of a falsely assumed rigidity of structure. It is in resolving some of the questions about the flexibility of existing constraints to human intervention, social or technological, and the dangers of creating new constraints that we believe models to have a role. The extraction of such information through detailed analysis relies on developments such as systematic and efficient statistical tools. In this respect the questions we have raised concerning the difficulties of calibrating and testing complex models are far from trivial.

To achieve *perfection* in forecasting may be impossible or incompatible with other social requirements, or even undesirable. Even if all existing constraints regarding theory, data and technique could be overcome, many questions would remain. We have seen that precise deterministic forecasting is impossible, particularly in the social field. In this sense, computer models can never give us a precise account of the future. Thus, although there is a challenge to modellers, systems analysts and others to develop better social forecasting methods and better means for displaying the uncertainty inherent in forecasting, this is not the ultimate goal, which is presumably to indicate the way to socially worthwhile futures.

A rather careful compromise with regard to technique and presentation has to be constructed to achieve the best forecasting performance taking into account all constraints and considerations. One certainly should not reject a method because of intrinsic barriers, especially when they are not fatal. It seems to us not sensible, even dangerous, that only one method should be prescribed or that any one method should be neglected; and, despite the deficiencies which we have described, we would consider that for some purposes large computer models have clear advantages over other methods for examining certain aspects of world problems. One valuable feature of the technique is that, if the time and expertise are available, it seems to be particularly amenable to criticism, which, negative or positive, can be constructive and can lead to improvements.

We have often been critical of computer modelling, both in general terms and in relation to specific models, and we believe that such criticism is essential to advancement. Some systems analysts have an almost evangelical faith in the simultation modelling technique; we do not believe that this is justified, but welcome the existence of individuals who are prepared to 'stick their necks out', provided that they submit their work to full scrutiny. Only in this way can progress be made.

Appendix A Interactive Simulation Modelling

There is a large literature on interactive computer simulation techniques—Greenblat (1972), for example, lists over 150 references of items relevant to the use, evaluation and design of simulations and games in the social sciences. The literature reflects the lack of a consistent theoretical structure in terms of the context, potential, limitations, kinds of results obtainable, usefulness and relevance of the different approaches; and there are problems of definition: for example, gaming, interactive simulation and man–machine systems often refer to the same type of exercise. This impression of the literature is partially corroborated by Schran and Kumpf (1972) who contacted about 25 scientists in the United States (where it is estimated that 90% of the work in interactive simulation is being, and has been, carried out) in order to assess the state-of-the-art in urban and regional gaming.

It is useful here to clarify the terms which are most commonly used and which we have used in Chapter 5. In 'man–machine system experiments' people interact with computer models and each other via the computer. (See Parsons (1972) for a fuller description, as well as examples of many man–machine system experiments.) 'Interactive computing' includes all forms of communication with a computer where the operator can continuously adjust his communication to the computer. Communication is usually through a teletype terminal or visual display unit, with the response from the computer being on the same device or on a lineprinter. In 'gaming' there is an attempt to maximize a defined objective junction (e.g. increasing income) in competition with a computer algorithm, other people or a combination of both man and algorithm. In 'interactive simulation' characteristics of a model are revealed: parameters not easily quantified (e.g. human values, hopes, fears and aspirations) are estimated by 'experts' operating the model. (For a more extensive discussion of the terms involved in simulation modelling, see McLeod (1968).)

'Computer conferencing and networks' are used either to play games in interactive computer mode or to be interactive simulation models. In each case, the 'players' are at remote locations connected to a central computer over communication networks. The networks can also be used to pass data from one location to another independently of the game or interactive simulation model.

A description of the hardware and software requirements needed for a workable interactive simulation system is given by Tartar and Sampson (1973).

Despite confusion surrounding the terminology and the objectives of games, they have been used widely in one form or another in many disciplines and for many purposes (e.g. Laska, 1973; Eiloart and Searle, 1973). Schran and Kumpf (1972), in their survey, suggest that, beyond the use of games to stimulate personal involvement and to enhance interpersonal communication (and recreation), games could be used for:

(1) Agitation: motivation of specific population groups (mainly those that are under-represented in the planning process at present) to participate actively in the planning process.

(2) Education training: demonstration and communication of interdependences and processes within complex socio-economic–technical systems.

(3) Research: investigation of possible regularities of social behavioural components in the context of economic–technical systems.

(4) Planning: development of alternative planning concepts and strategies and testing their practicability.

They remark that most of the games they reviewed fall into the education and training category, with a few constructed for research and none for planning.

There is generally no detailed attempt in the literature to justify the use of games and, thus, generally no evidence is provided that such games should be encouraged other than for fun. The evidence that does exist is not encouraging, although in an annotated bibliography of games and simulations for teaching economics (in the main not computer-based) by Lewis and Wentworth (1971), a survey of work completed in the area showed that most researchers agreed that games and simulations did not statistically improve the learning of students when compared with traditional methods. However, motivation and attitudes noticeably changed. These results were partly corroborated by Chartier (1972).

It is possible that similar results would apply to other areas such as management business games or war games. However, despite the seeming disutility of games for education purposes, other commentators suggest it may be useful for helping policy makers to understand simulation models; for example, Richardson (1973) remarks that gaming (interactive simulation, by our definition) is seen as a principal means of integration between the policy maker and the model, although experiments in this direction have yet to be evaluated thoroughly.

The distinction between gaming and interactive simulation modelling is made here since the object of the most recent work in this field in world models and elsewhere (e.g. Mesarovic (1972) and Battelle (1972)) has been to simulate the behaviour of policy analysts or policy makers as part of a model and not to have opposing individuals or teams competing to maximize a particular objective. In the former type of model players must not only maximize their own objective functions but must also be subject to the constraint that the 'welfare' of the other players should not be unduly disrupted. In this way, variables and objective functions defying quantification are crudely incorporated.

Again it is difficult to provide evidence that such simulations will be useful for policy making. Richardson (1973) remarks:

Gaming has been used to examine the behaviour of decision makers, to develop theories about decision processes and to sensitize decision makers (and others) to the complexities of large systems (Ray and Duke, 1968), but has not been extensively used (or even widely discussed) as a potential for policy analysis [although suggests that the most notable among the exceptions to this generalization is the work of Peter House, Environmental Studies Division of the Office of Research and Monitoring, Environmental Protection Agency]. The obvious rationale for linking an interactive mode decision stratum to large models is that it allows the decision maker and the computer to work as partners in analysing the decision situation, with each assuming an assigned role which will use the capabilities of both most advantageously.

Mesarovic and coworkers (1973a) are more optimistic:

In interactive mode operation, the anlysis is the outcome of both the logical and computing capabilities of the machine on the one hand and the intuition, experience and heuristic capabilities of man on the other. Such a symbiosis avoids the pitfalls of relying solely on the computer for policy analysis, which by necessity leads to a mechanistic view of the situation; it provides also means for creative use of computer techniques for extending the logical capability of man in long-term planning and analysis while preserving the ultimate responsibility for prediction, planning and decision making in his hands.

An upsurge of interest in computer conferencing has recently occurred in the US (see, for example, Krend (1973), Richardson (1973), Noel (1973), Turoff (1972) and Utsumi (1973)). Richardson (1973), one of the collaborators on the Mesarovic–Pestel model, suggests that the structure of the model makes the use of 'multiple interactors and computer communication not only desirable, but probably essential'. He suggests that, since there is no one client for a world model, if the model is to achieve its purposes, it must gain acceptance as a tool by individuals whose responsibility it is to actually set goals and implement policies rather than to merely speculate about them. He hopes that such an objective can be achieved by physically locating a family of regional models on computers situated in the regions being modelled and by linking the computers using communication satellites; decision makers could simultaneously set goals for their respective regions, observe the responses from other regions and work at the implications of alternative scenarios.

The small amount of evidence, then, suggests that simulation gaming does not, surprisingly, aid the education process of individuals significantly and only marginally increases their motivation. Again, although it is possible that forecasting will be improved by incorporating people interactively 'inside a model', the impossibility of their having a representative set of values or aspirations means that such interactive simulations (including gaming) may have merit only in serving as an interface between a researcher and the model. Nevertheless, this process should help improve the understanding that the user has of both the limitations and the uses of the model.

Although interactive simulation models may add another dimension for policy makers to both understand a model and to test ideas out interactively with a model, the current state of modelling does not suggest to us that many models correspond to the real world accurately enough to be useful for policy testing or for their policy formulation. Thus computing conferencing networks may well be the result of modellers being carried away with the glamour of their tools.

Appendix B Technical Tools of Modelling

This section is concerned almost entirely with computers, languages and the interaction of the issues considered in Chapter 5 with the choice of computer and language.

Computers are essentially information processors of a simple form. Today, thirty years after they first became generally available, they still consist, in the digital form unarguably, of five elements, i.e. INPUT, MEMORY, LOGIC, ARITHMETIC, OUTPUT. Today's computers only differ from those of thirty years ago in that these five elements are now fully interconnectable and can carry multiple streams of independent (but not interdependent) data at ever-increasing speeds. Unfortunately, however, in spite of the nominal attempts to achieve relocatability of a program from one machine to another, the wide variety of different machine configurations and intimate-software patterns has meant that instant relocatability has receded further into the future. This has implications for the checking of models by independent peer groups. The same is true for the choice of languages discussed below.

The choice of machine ranges from pure digital, through hybrid, to pure analog computers. Digital computers in the main are used by simulation modellers. In principle they are not limited by size of model and can be made as precise as required; and many programming languages even have internally adjustable precision. There is plenty of available expertise. They can carry out repetitive calculations and, once successfully loaded, can go through innumerable trajectories, but at high (though false) 'cost'. In contrast, analog computers are restricted in size and rather imprecise, with about 1% accuracy for an individual subsystem and 5% accuracy for an overall system. They have a comparatively low threshold time to access, but expertise is lacking and control (though easier) requires much more human supervision to implement. Most simulation languages for digital machines attempt to incorporate the interaction benefits of analog computing.

Since all the world models we have discussed employ digital machines we will restrict comment to the various simulation programming facilities available for these. Many articles have been written about various simulation languages. Dealing with continuous system simulation languages (CSSLs) alone, and ignoring discrete simulation languages and hybrid continuous–discrete mixtures, the authors found nearly three score different languages in extensive use in the UK alone. What then are some of the criteria sought, and which should be sought, in a CSSL?

CSSLs have not been used extensively in the simulation of social systems, the languages having been developed, in the main, for the simulation of physical and engineering systems. CSSLs are used in preference to 'high-level' languages such as FORTRAN or ALGOL since they were built especially for the simulation of continuous systems, i.e. those systems characterizable by ordinary differential equations in one or more independent variables. Their development was further motivated by the need to reduce the task of programming the digital computer and the requirement of providing flexibility in changing the parameters of a simulation experiment.

The savings achieved by CSSLs are not without drawbacks, since they have been achieved at the expense of increased computer time and, to a certain extent, programming flexibility. Further, it is unusual for one team of workers, in a fixed computing environment, to be adept at more than one CSSL.

Based on our experience with the simulation of social systems and the remarks made above, the minimum standards for a CSSL designed to simulate a social system are considered to be the following (largely adapted from the CSSL report of Nilsen and Karplus (1973)):

(1) Easily understood by programmers unfamiliar with digital computer techniques, i.e. problem orientated operator set.

(2) Has a subset and manual which can introduce programmers gradually to the language (particularly important to social scientist users).

(3) Applicable to all scientific computers (i.e. its compiler preferably written in a high-level language such as FORTRAN IV).

(4) A minimal set of operators capable of handling most problems involving differential equations.

(5) Preprogrammed integration routines plus a facility to allow the user to incorporate his own integration routine and historical lags.

(6) Preprogrammed input and output functions (especially graphical output).

(7) Between-run control of parameters.

(8) Problem orientated diagnostics (compilation and run time), especially for variables used but not defined and vice versa.

(9) Inclusion of a SORT feature to allow non-procedural definition of parallel dynamic regions.

(10) CSSL should be an adjunct to an established procedural language such as FORTRAN IV (FORTRAN IV should be a subset of the CSSL).

(11) The operator set should be open-ended with simple procedures for introducing user-generated operators.

(12) Should incorporate built-in subroutine functions and should also allow user defined subroutines (macros).

(13) Should provide a block-diagram language along the lines of most digital–analog simulators.

(14) Should provide for flexible expansion to accommodate advances in computer organization such as graphic displays, interactive terminals, conversational mode programming and others.

(15) No problem size restriction, e.g. overlaying should be allowed.

The situation with regard to CSSLs is far from satisfactory from the point of view of the modelling community as a whole, since, even if an individual modeller is happy with a particular language, it is difficult for him to run his model on another machine due to the lack of standardization. However, it is encouraging to note that most of the languages conform approximately to the standards laid down in the CSSL report quoted above, with many far surpassing its recommendations (e.g. ASL, CSMP III, SPEED and SLAM). With the restriction on the number of equations in SPEED and the lack of an interactive form of SLAM, ASL and CSMP III seem to be the most versatile. DYNAMO lacks many of these optional facilities.

The leaning of the CSSL report was towards the simulation of scientific and engineering systems. Thus it is particularly difficult for social scientists, for example, to become quickly familiar with the present generation of simulation languages, with the possible exception of DYNAMO. Also, because of the increased difficulties in simulating social systems in comparison to biological or physical systems, the social scientist has different requirements to those that the scientists or engineers have traditionally demanded. Thus, owing to the practical impossibility of building accurate models of social systems, the modeller of these systems must use the available simulation languages and computer hardware more as a sketchpad for ideas. To achieve such more limited objectives, the social system modeller needs, perversely, easy-to-use interactive facilities as well as a language which can be manipulated easily. This latter requirement should not preclude the desired language from having advanced features, as long as their explanation and documentation do not swamp the inexperienced user.

Finally, in view of the apparent universality of the System Dynamics (SD) approach, as advocated by Forrester (1971b), the following observations are pertinent. Nonlinearities can be introduced in the approach, if the DYNAMO language is used, in two ways. Rate equations specifying rates of change introduce nonlinearities, and the table function representation of intra-variable relationships readily lends itself to nonlinear forms. DYNAMO and SD *need not* introduce nonlinearities. The ease with which nonlinearities can be introduced has led to a proliferation of large nonlinear models. Such models are apparently 'transparent', although as discussed in Chapter 5 their behaviour is analytically intractable. Nevertheless, there is an argument (discussed elsewhere) that, phenomenologically, they may be used to capture the current behaviour of a 'complex' system.

The simplicity and appeal of the System Dynamics method of representation is such that many people, previously unfamiliar with complex models or complex representations, can contribute to the SD flowchart representation with ease. It is only in the later stages of calibration, inference and validation that the enormous difficulty of building an accepted quantitative SD model, rather than a phenomenological one, can be appreciated (the MIT models illustrate this point well).

References

Ackoff, R. L. (1960), 'Systems, organizations, and interdisciplinary research', *General Systems*, **V**, pp. 1–8.

Ackoff, R. L. (1962), *Scientific Method: Optimizing Applied Research Decisions*, Wiley.

Ackoff, R. L. (1971), 'Towards a system of systems concepts', *Management Science*, **17**, 11.

Adams, J. (1973), 'Everything under control', *Science for People*, No. 21, April/May 1973.

Allen, V. (1973), Inaugural Lecture, University of Leeds, *Times Higher Educational Supplement*, 8th February 1974.

Armytage, W. H. (1965), *The Rise of the Technocrats*, Routledge and Kegan Paul, London.

Arrow, K. J. (1957), 'Mathematical models in the social sciences', in D. R. Lerner and D. D. Lasswell (Eds.), *The Policy Sciences*, Stanford University Press.

Ash, J. C. and Smyth, D. J. (1974), *Forecasting the U.K. Economy*, Saxon House.

Ashby, Lord (1973), in Jahoda (1973b).

Ball, R. J. (1967), 'Econometric models', *Mathematical Model Building in Economics and Industry*, Griffin, London.

Barras, R. and coworkers (1971), 'An operational urban development model of Cheshire', *Environment and Planning*, Vol. 3, pp. 109–242.

Battelle (1972), 'DEMATEL: 1972 Report' (mimeo).

Beckerman, W. (1972), 'Economists, scientists and environmental catastrophe', Inaugural lecture at University College, London, (mimeo).

Beer, S. (1972), *The Brain of the Firm*, Allen Lane.

Beer, S. (1973), *Fanfare for Effective Freedom*, Allen Lane.

Bellman, R. (1971), 'Mathematics, systems and society', FEK Report, Stockholm.

Benyon, P. R. (1972), 'Computer modelling and interdisciplinary teams', *Search*, **3**, 7.

Bertalanffy, L. Von (1969), *General Systems Theory: Essays on its Foundation and Development*, Braziller.

Blankenship, G. and coworkers (1974), 'Construction of regionalized world economic model—Vol. 1' (mimeo).

Blauner, A. (1960), in W. Galenson and S. M. Lipset (Eds.), *Labour and Trade Unionism*, Wiley.

Bohm, D. (1957), *Causality and Chance in Modern Physics*, Routledge and Kegan Paul.

Borgesse, E. M. (1973), 'The activities of the International Ocean Institute', Report to the Club of Rome.

Bottomore, T. B. and Rubel, M. (1956), *Karl Marx—Selected Writings in Sociology and Social Philosophy*, Penguin.

Boulding, K. E. (1956), 'General systems theory: the skeleton of science', *Management Science*, April, pp. 197–208.

Box, G. E. P. and Jenkins, G. M. (1970), *Time-Series Analysis: Forecasting and Control*, Holden Day.

Boyd, R. (1972), 'World Dynamics—a note' *Science*, **177**, August, 516–519

Bray, J. (1972), 'A model of doom', *Nature*, **238**, 5359, 112.

Brehm, J. (1970), *Theory of Psychological Reactants*, Academic Press.

Brewer, G. D. (1973), '*Politicians, Bureaucrats and the Consultant*', Basic Books.

Brewer, G. D. and Hall, O. P. (1973), *Policy Analysis by Computer Simulation: The Need for Appraisal*, Rand.

Broadbent, T. A. (1973), 'An approach to the application of urban models in the planning system of the U.K.', Conference on Dynamic Allocation in Space, Stockholm.

Burke, E. (1973), 'Ignorance about limitation to growth', *Nature*, **246**, 23rd November, pp. 226–230.

Burnett, R. A. and Dionne, P. J. (1973), 'GLOBE 6: A multiregion interactive world simulation', *Simulation*, June.

Carson, R. (1962), *Silent Spring*, Riverside Press.

Cellarius, R and Platt, J. L. (1972), 'Council of urgent studies', *Science*, 25 August, pp. 670–676.

Chaney, R. (1972), in D. L. Clarke (Ed.) *Models in Archaeology*, Methuen.

Chartier, M. (1972), 'Learning effect—an experimental study of a simulation game and instrumental discussion', *Simulation and Games*, **3**, 3.

Checkland, P. B. (1971), 'A systems map of the universe', *Journal of Systems Engineering*, **2**, 2.

Chisholm, A. (1972). *Philosophers of the Earth—Conversations with Ecologists*, Sidgwick and Jackson.

Chorley, R. and Haggett, H. (1967), *Models in Geography*, Methuen.

Clark, J. A. and coworkers (1973), 'A feasibility study for a socio-economic model of Europe', EEC (Brussels) DG XII, June (mimeo).

Clark, J. A. and coworkers (1974), 'Experimental models of Europe', *Futures*, December.

Clymer, A. (1969), 'The modelling and simulation of big systems', *Simulation and Modelling Conference*, Pittsburg, p. 107.

Cole, H. S. D. (1974), 'Technological forecasting and problems of dependency', background paper to UNCTAD/UNEP Group on Environment and Development.

Cole, H. S. D. and Curnow, R. C. (1973), 'Backcasting with the world models', *Nature*, 18th March.

Cole, H. S. D and coworkers (1973), *Thinking About the Future*, Chatto and Windus.

Cottrell, A. (1973), 'Problems of predicting future world trends', *Nature*, **245**, October 12.

Council of Europe, (1973), 'Long range forecasting and regional planning', background papers CEMAT (73) 1, 2, 8, 12.

Crawford, M. (1974) *Sunday Times*, 28 April.

Cuypers, J. (1972), *World Dynamics—Two Simplified Versions of Forrester's Model*, Eindhoven University of Technology.

Curry, L. (1972), 'A spatial analysis of gravity flows', *Regional Studies*, **6**, 131–147.

Dator, J. (1972), 'Outline of the past and future stages in the development of the West Hawaii Model Project' (mimeo).

Dator, J. (1974), 'Neither here, there nor then', in *Human Futures*, IPC.

Eiloart, T. and Searle, N. (1973), 'Business games off the shelf', *Simulation*, **20**, 2.

Encel, S. and coworkers (1975), *The Art of Anticipation*, (to be published by Martin Robertson).

EPA (Environmental Protection Agency) (1971), 'Estuary modelling: an assessment', *Water Pollution Control Series 17070, DZV 02/7*.

FAO (1967), *Agricultural Commodities—Projections for 1975 and 1985*, Vols. I and II, FAO, Rome.

Feyerabend, P. (1970), in I. Lakatos (Ed.), 'Criticism and the growth of knowledge', Proceedings of the International Colloquium in the Philosophy of Science.

Flexner, A. (1930), *Universities American, English, German*, Oxford University Press, New York.

Forrester, J. W. (1969), *Urban Dynamics*, MIT.

Forrester, J. W. (1971a), *World Dynamics*, MIT.

Forrester, J. W. (1971b) 'On the counterintuitive behaviour of social systems', *Technology Review*, **73**, 3.

Forrester, J. W. and coworkers (1974), 'The debate on "World Dynamics"—a response to Nordhaus, *Policy Science*, June.

Freeman, C. (1971), 'Technology assessment and its social context', *Studium Generale*, **24.**

Gardner, M. and Ashby, W. R. (1970), 'Connectance of large dynamic (cybernetic) systems: critical values for stability', *Nature*, **228,** November 21.

Gillette, R. (1972), 'Hard sell for a computer view of Doomsday', *Science*, March.

Graham, F., Jr. (1970), *Since 'Silent Spring'*, Pan Books.

Greenblat, C. S. (1972), 'Gaming and simulation in the social sciences—a guide to the literature', *Simulation and Games*, December.

Hamilton H. R. and coworkers (1969), *Systems Simulation for Regional Analysis—An Application to River-Basin Planning*, MIT.

Hart, H. (1959), 'Social theory and social change', in L. Cross (Ed.) *Symposium on Sociological Theory*, Harper and Row.

Herrera, A. (1973), 'Latin American world model: progress report', (mimeo).

Hesse, M. (1966), *Models and Analogies in Science*, University of Notre Dame Press.

Hickman, B. G. and coworkers (1970), 'Background, organisations and preliminary results of Project LINK', Second World Congress of Economic Society, Cambridge.

Hoos, I. (1969), *Systems Analysis in Social Policy*, Institute of Economic Affairs.

Hoos, I. (1972), *Systems Analysis in Public Policy—A Critique*, University of California Press.

House, P. W. (1973), 'Environmental modelling vs the "chicken soup" approach', *Simulation*, June.

House, P. W. and Tyndall, G. R. (1973), 'Models and policy making' (mimeo).

Howells, G. (1973), 'The ecological challenge of estuaries', *Environment and Change*, November.

Hyrenius, A. (1973), 'On the use of models as instruments in forming population policies', paper prepared for UN Conference on Population.

Ishitani, H. (1973), in Kaya and coworkers (1973a).

Jahoda, M. (1973a), 'Forecasting: dilemmas and assumptions', SPRU (mimeo).

Jahoda, M. (1973b), 'Thinking about the future', *Times Higher Educational Supplement*, 22nd June.

Jansson, B. O. (1972), *Ecosystem Approach to the Baltic Problem*, University of Stockholm.

Jeffers, J. N. R. (1973), 'Systems modelling and analysis in resource management', *Journal of Environmental Management*, **1,** 1.

Jenkins, G. M. (1969), 'The systems approach', *Journal of Engineering Systems*, **1,** 1.

Kahn, H. and Weiner, A. J. (1967), 'The Year Two Thousand', Collier-Macmillan.

Kajona, J. (1973), 'The problem of aggregation in location models', *Conference on Dynamic Allocation in Space*, Stockholm, *1973*.

Kaldor, N. (1970), *Conflicts in National Economic Objectives*, Oxford.

Kast F. E. and Rosenzweig, J. E. (1970), *Organization and Management: A Systems Approach*, McGraw–Hill.

Kaya, Y. and Suzuki, Y. (1974), 'Global constraints and a new vision for development—II', *Technological Forecasting and Social Change*, **6,** pp. 371–388.

Kaya, Y. and coworkers (1973a), *On the Future Japan and the World—A Model Approach*, Japan Techno-Economics Society.

Kaya, Y. and coworkers (1973b), *Towards a Global Vision of Human Problems*, Japan Techno-Economics Society.

Kaysen, C. (1972), 'The computer that printed out WOLF', *Foreign Affairs*, **50,** 4.

Kennedy, M. C. (1969), 'How well does the National Institute forecast?', *National Institute Economic Review*, November.

Ketchum, B. H. (1972), *The Water's Edge*, MIT Press.

King, A. (1974), 'The Club of Rome today', *Simulation in the Service of Society*, August.

Krauch, H. (1973), 'Direct decision-making by the people', University of Heidelberg (mimeo).

Krend, J. (1973), 'Adapting complex man-machine simulations for network gaming—an extended summary', Montreal, Summer Computer Simulation Conference.

Kruskal, J. (1965), *Journal of the Royal Statistical Society*, B, p. 251.

Kuhn, T. S. (1962), *The Structure of Scientific Revolutions*, University of Chicago.

Lambert, J. (1972), 'Growth and politics', *Agenor*, April/May.

Laska, R. M. (1973), 'The river basin model-player's guide', report of the Environmental Protection Agency.

Lee, D. B. (1972), 'Requiem for large scale models' (mimeo).

Lee, D. B. (1973), 'Requiem for large scale models', *AIP Journal*, May.

Lewis, D. R. and Wentworth, D. (1971), *Games and Simulations for Teaching Economics*, Joint Council on Economic Education.

Lindblom, C. (1959), 'The science of "muddling through"', *Public Administration Review*, **19.**

Lindblom, C. and Hirshman, A. (1962), 'Economic development, research and development, policy making: some converging views', *Behavioural Science*, **7.**

Linnemann, H. (1973), Report to the Club of Rome on the Project 'Problems of Population Doubling' (mimeo).

Little, A. D. (1966), 'Model of the San Francisco housing market', Arthur D. Little *Technical Paper no. 8.*

Lowe, P. (1972), 'Problems Progress: Some answers to questions on project "Yearbook of World Problems"' (mimeo).

Lowry, I. S. (1964), *A Model of Metropolis*, Rand Corporation.

Mar, B. and Newell, W. T. (1973), 'An assement of selected RANN environmental modelling efforts' (mimeo).

Margalef, R. (1968), *Perspectives in Ecological Theory*, University of Chicago Press.

Marstrand, P. and Sinclair, C. (1973), in Cole and coworkers (1973).

Massey, D. B. and Cordey-Hayes, M. (1971), 'The use of models in structure planning', *Town Planning Review*, **42,** (1).

Maynard-Smith, J. (1974), *Models in Ecology*, Cambridge.

McClelland, C. and coworkers (1971), 'The management and analysis of event data', Los Angeles University, California.

McLeod, J. (Ed) (1968), *Simulation: The Modelling of Ideas and Systems with Computers*, McGraw–Hill.

Meadows, D. and coworkers (1972), *The Limits to Growth*, Universe Books and Earth Island.

Meadows, D. and coworkers (1973), 'Response to Sussex', *Futures* **1,** February.

Mesarovic, M. (1970), *Theory of Multilevel Hierarchical Systems*, Academic Press.

Mesarovic, M. (1972), 'A goal seeking and regionalised model for analysis of critical world relationships—the conceptual foundation, *Kybernetics*, **1,** 79–85.

Mesarovic, M. and coworkers (1973a), 'An interactive decision stratum for the multilevel world model' (mimeo.) See also *Futures*, August, 357–366.

Mesarovic, M. and coworkers (1973b), 'Regionalised and adaptive model of the global world system' (mimeo).

Mesarovic, M. and Pestel, E. (1974a), *Mankind at the Turning Point*, E. P. Dutton & Co. Readers Digest Press.

Mesarovic, M. and coworkers (1974b), 'Multilevel world model project', IIASA, Vienna, May 1974 (mimeo).

Mihram, G. (1973), 'The publication of simulation models' (mimeo).

Mitroff, I. I. and Turoff, M. (1973), 'Technological forecasting and assessment: science and/or mythology', *Technological Forecasting and Social Change*, **5,** 2.

Miyakoda, K. (1974), 'Numerical weather production', *American Scientist*, **62,** pp. 564–574.

Nelson, R. (1974), 'Intellectualising about the Moon-Ghetto metaphor: a study of the current malaise of rational analysis of social problems', *Policy Sciences*, **5,** pp. 375–415.

Nilsen, R. and Karplus, W. (1973), 'Continuous System Simulation Languages: A state of the art survey', (mimeo).

Noel, R. C. (1973), 'POLIS—and network simulation', *Simulation in the Service of Society*, **3**, 1.

Nordbeck, B. (1971), 'Problem: What is a problem?', *International Associations*, **7**, 405–408

Nordhaus, W. D. (1973), 'World dynamics—measurement without data', *Economic Journal*, December.

NSF (National Science Foundation) (1974), 'Federally supported mathematical models' (mimeo).

OECD (1969), Agricultural projections for 1975 and 1985, OECD, Paris.

OECD (1972), *Analytical Methods in Government Science Policy* (Science Policy Series, OECD).

Odum, H. T. (1972), *Ecology*, Holt.

Oerlemans, T. and coworkers (1972), 'World dynamics: social feedback may give hope for the future', *Nature*, **238.**

Page, W. (1973), in Cole and coworkers (1973).

Parsons, H. M. (1972), *Man–Machine System Experiments*, Johns Hopkins Press.

Pavitt, K. (1972), 'Analytic techniques in government science policy', *Futures*, March.

Peccei, A. (1969), *The Chasm Ahead*, Macmillan, London.

Peccei, A. (1973a), 'The Club of Rome—the new threshold', *Simulation*, **20**, 6.

Peccei, A. (1973b), 'The moment of truth is approaching', *Successo*, December.

Peterson, J J. (1973), 'Energy and the weather', *Environment*, **15**, pp. 4–9.

Popper, K. R. (1963), *Conjectures and Refutations: The Growth of Scientific Knowledge*, Routledge and Kegan Paul.

Prigogine, I. and coworkers (1972), 'The thermodynamics of evolution', *Physics Today*, **25**, 11.

Rademaker, O. (1974), 'Project group global dynamics—Report no. 4' (mimeo).

Ramo, S. (1969), *Cure for Chaos: Fresh Solutions to Social Problems through the Systems Approach*, McKay.

Rapoport, A. (1959), 'Uses and limitations of mathematical models in social science', in L. Gross (Ed.), *Symposium on Sociological Theory*, Harper and Row.

Ray, P. H. and Duke, R. D. (1968), 'The environment of decision-makers in urban gaming simulation', in W. Coplin (Ed.), *Simulation in the Study of Politics*, University of Chicago Press.

Ray, D. and coworkers (1973), 'A dynamic model of health and socio-economic development' (mimeo).

Richardson, J. M. (1973), 'Gaming simulation using computer communication as a tool for policy analysis: a brief from the Devil's Advocate', *SRC Tech. Memo. 49*.

Roberts, P. (1973), 'Models of the future' *Omega*, **1**, 5.

Saito, S. (1973), in Kaya and coworkers (1973a).

Sayer, A. (1974), 'A dynamic Lowry model' in M. H. Whithed and R. M. Sarly (Eds.) *Urban Simulation: Models for Public Policy Analysis* (Nato Advanced Study Series).

Schrin, H. and Kumpf, D. (1972), 'Environmental games in the United States—a review of a decade of confusion', *Simulation and Games*, December.

Schultze, C. L. (1968), *The Politics and Economics of Public Spending*, Brookings.

Scolnik, H. (1973), 'On a methodological criticism of meadows' World 3 model' (mimeo).

Sears, S. W. (1973), 'The use of simulation in the field of urban and regional planning', *Simulation Today*, No. 13.

Sharp, J. (1974), 'A study of some problems of system dynamics methodology', Ph.D. thesis, University of Bradford.

Sharpe, R. and Brotchie, J. F. (1973), *An Urban Systems Study*, Bridge Printing Pty. Ltd., NSW.

Simmons, H. (1973), in Cole and coworkers (1973).

Sinclair, T. C. (1973), in Cole and coworkers (1973).

Stevenage, (1972), 'Mathematical and hydraulic modelling of estuarine pollution', *Water Pollution Research Laboratory Technical Papers*.

Tanter, R. (1972), 'The policy relevance of models in world politics', *Journal of Conflict Resolution*, **XVI**, 4.

Tartar, J. and Sampson (1973), 'Requirements for interactive simulation systems', *Simulation*, May.

Thiemann, H. (1973a), Report on Battelle's activities to the Club of Rome, Tokyo.

Thiemann, H. (1973b), interview in *Europhysics News*, August.

Thomas, J. (1974), 'Models as an aid to policy making', *New Scientist*, 7th February.

Tinker, J. (1972), 'Britain to start a limits-to-growth unit', *New Scientist*, 15th June.

Turoff, M. (1972), 'Party line and discussion—computerised conference systems', *ISP Proceedings*, April.

United Nations (1968), *Development in the Construction and Use of Macro-Economic Models*, UN, New York.

Utsumi, T. (1973), 'Systems development for global gaming simulation', presented at: 1973 International Symposium on Computers and Chinese L/O systems, August, Taipei, Taiwan.

Van der Grinten, P.M.E.M. and de Jong, P. J. (1971), 'Werelddynamica gezien vammit de system on regetechniek' *Chemisch Weekblad*, December

Watt, K. E. G. (1968), *Ecology and Resource Management: A Quantiative Approach*, McGraw–Hill.

Watt, K. and coworkers (1973), *Land Use, Energy Flow and Decision Making in Human Society*, NSF GI–27.

Ways, M. (1962), 'The road to 1977', in F. E. Emery (Ed.) *System Thinking*, Penguin.

Weinberg, A. N. (1967), *Reflections on Big Science*, MIT Press.

Wéry, R., Rodgers, G. B., and Hopkins, M. D. (1974), 'BACHUE-2: version I—a population and employment model for the Phillipines' *Population and Employment Project Working Paper 5*, ILO Geneva.

Williams, E. R. and House, P. W. (1973), *The State of the System* (SOS) *Model*, EPA Washington, R 5–73.

Wilson, A (1970), *Entropy in Urban and Regional Modelling*, Pion.

World Bank (1973), Haq and coworkers 'Report on *The Limits to Growth*' (mimeo).

Wright, M. J. (1973), 'Retrodictive tests of systems dynamics models', *Proceedings* of the Summer Simulation Conference.

Young, P. (1973), paper presented at the Warwick Conference on Modelling National Economics.

Zeman, M. (1973), 'Action against the future' (mimeo).

Index